HUNTING THE GRISLY AND
OTHER SKETCHES

HUNTING THE GRISLY AND OTHER SKETCHES

An Account of the Big Game of the United States,
and Its Chase with Horse, Hound, and Rifle

Theodore Roosevelt

Introduction by Stephanie Nikolopoulos

BARNES
&NOBLE
BOOKS
NEW YORK

CONTENTS

INTRODUCTION   VII

I. THE BISON OR AMERICAN BUFFALO   1

II. THE BLACK BEAR   20

III. OLD EPHRAIM, THE GRISLY BEAR   28

IV. HUNTING THE GRISLY   51

V. THE COUGAR   80

VI. A PECCARY HUNT ON THE NUECES   90

VII. HUNTING WITH HOUNDS   99

VIII. WOLVES AND WOLF-HOUNDS   118

IX. IN COWBOY LAND   137

ENDNOTES   165

SUGGESTED READING   167

INTRODUCTION

WRITTEN by the man the teddy bear is named after, *Hunting the Grisly and Other Sketches* brilliantly captures the thrill of the chase as Theodore Roosevelt recounts his North-American hunting adventures. Told in campfire-story spirit, it is a celebration of the great outdoors, a handbook on hunting, and a socio-historical record of the United States in the nineteenth century.

An asthmatic who grew up in New York City, Theodore Roosevelt (1858-1919) seemed an unlikely candidate for wild game hunting. Because Roosevelt was confined to the house as a child due to his asthma, "he would read adventure stories," according to National Park Service Rangers at the Theodore Roosevelt Birthplace National Historic Site. As he grew up, he "started living his own adventure stories." Through a strict exercise regimen he overcame his initial frailties and grew into the revered sportsman whose conservationist efforts led to the establishment of America's greatest game preserves. His survival skills were honed as a Rough Rider in the Spanish-American War, and his demonstrated leadership paved the path for him to become twenty-sixth president of the United States of America, a profession that seemed to be in his genes given that his cousin was Franklin Delano Roosevelt.

By instinctively writing about the great game animals of the West, Theodore Roosevelt preserved the untamable spirit of America during the nineteenth and early twentieth century. As the United States' fascination with the Wild West grew—in 1803 Lewis and Clark began their great adventure, and by 1845 the

phrase "Manifest Destiny" had been coined by John O'Sullivan—
pioneers' impact on nature was visible. When "Buffalo Bill" Cody
ushered in the mass slaughtering of the bison, even Roosevelt purchased ranches in the Dakota Badlands aspiring to add to his
hunting collection this symbol of the West before it became
extinct. Not surprisingly, buffalo hunting is the very first chapter
in *Hunting the Grisly* and is discussed in relation to the transconti-
nental railroad. Roosevelt attributed his experiences in the
Badlands to his later success; when President William McKinley
was assassinated in 1901—ironically in *Buffalo,* New York—
Theodore Roosevelt, his running mate during his second term,
became president. A year later he had ratified the Newlands
Reclamation Act, which promoted Western settlement.

As settlers continued to move West, hunting wild game served a
dual purpose: political—it forced Native Americans, whose survival
depended on the natural resources (buffalo "furnished all the
means of livelihood to [some] tribes," according to *Hunting the Grisly*)
to relocate so that white settlers could claim their territory—and
sport—it promoted outdoor adventure and competition. While
his earlier book *The Winning of the West* pits man against man (it
reflects Roosevelt's view that "The settler ousts no one from the
land. The truth is, the Indians never had any real title to the soil"),
Hunting the Grisly focuses on the age-old battle of man versus
nature. Although hunting for sport is today oftentimes viewed as
problematic, if not blood thirsty, because of the rapid deforestation
of the country and the adding of grizzlies to the endangered list in
1975, one must view *Hunting the Grisly* in the cultural context of the
era. Hunting was the extreme sport of the nineteenth century,
somewhat like skydiving is today, and the vivid passages in *Hunting
the Grisly* relate the daring exploits of facing North America's most
cunning creatures. "During the years I lived on the frontier I came
in contact with many persons who had been severely mauled or
even crippled for life by grislies," asserts Roosevelt. "Sometimes a
single bite causes death," he reveals about the grizzly bear, which
he calls the "king of the game beasts."

Having his article "Hunting the Grisly" appear in the popular hunting and fishing magazine *Field & Stream* in January 1899, Roosevelt stands on his own as a hunter. Subtitled *An Account of the Big Game of the United States, and Its Chase with Horse, Hound, and Rifle*, the book, like the magazine article, offers expert advice in the varied tools and methods of hunting. Roosevelt, whose fellow Rough Rider William Tiffany was the son of the founder of Tiffany & Company, had his hunting equipment fashioned at the famous jewelry store and later had his equipment for his African safari provided by Abercrombie & Fitch, the same retailer that outfitted several other presidents, as well as Amelia Earhart and Ernest Hemingway. The first rifle Roosevelt owned was a thirty-eight caliber Ballard. A marksman and a National Rifle Association Life Member, Roosevelt later "signed Public Law 149 into effect, authorizing the sale, at cost, of surplus military rifles, ammunition, and related equipment to rifle clubs meeting requirements specified by the [National Board for the Promotion of Rifle Practice] and approved by the Secretary of War," according to the NRA Institute for Legislative Action.

Besides hunting with a rifle, Roosevelt also hunted with dogs, some of which were "descendants of Custer's hounds." In *Hunting the Grisly*, Roosevelt explains that "as the old wilderness hunter type passes away, hounds come into use among his successors, the rough border settlers of the backwoods and the plains." He gives some insight into popular breeds and the regional differences in using dogs on hunts, and says, "of all sports possible in civilized countries, riding to hounds is perhaps the best if followed as it should be, for the sake of the strong excitement, with as much simplicity as possible, and not merely as a fashionable amusement. It tends to develop moral no less than physical qualities; the rider needs nerve and head; he must possess daring and resolution, as well as a good deal of bodily skill and a certain amount of wiry toughness and endurance."

At the Theodore Roosevelt Birthplace National Historic Site, there is, in addition to the reconstructed birthplace, a gallery called the "Lion's Room," which displays more than a dozen heads and pelts—including two birds that Roosevelt mounted himself and the head of a bear. Roosevelt presented many of these hunting trophies to his wife and adorned the White House with some of them. National Park Service Rangers point out that they "taxidermied animals back then with arsenic," and "used the brains of the animal to tan the skin." These hunting tools and practices snap to life in *Hunting the Grisly* as Roosevelt describes men disastrously getting caught in the traps they set, wolves overcoming one dog only to succumb to the pack, and horses escaping the wrath of the great grizzly.

In fact, what makes Roosevelt's book stand out from others on hunting is this masterful pairing of expertise with high literary quality. *Hunting the Grisly* is nuzzled in the tradition of Davy Crockett, who in *Bear Hunting in Tennessee* (1834), boasts "one hundred and five bears I had killed in less than one year," and Thomas Bangs Thorpe, who in *The Big Bear of Arkansans* (1854) recognizes the diminishing population of animals that Western civilization has fraught, and even Winslow Homer, who in the painting *Bear Hunting, Prospect Rock* (1892) portrays wild game hunting. On the whole, the popular literature of the early nineteenth century—the works of James Fenimore Cooper (*The Deerslayer*), Henry David Thoreau (*Walden*), and Walt Whitman (*Leaves of Grass*)—concerned itself thematically with man's relationship with nature.

Nature references and particularly hunting passages have increasingly been replaced by urban and technological metaphor in North-American writing, but Roosevelt's intimations of nature persist in contemporary bestsellers, like acclaimed travel writer Bill Bryson's *A Walk in the Woods: Rediscovering America on the Appalachian Trail* (1998), the opening chapter of which reflects the spine-tingling anticipation of coming in contact with the grizzly while hiking through the forests of the United States. Even at the turn of the millennium, when scores of writers throughout the centuries could have overshadowed Roosevelt, his writing was so memorable that it stood up alongside Ivan Turgenev and Ernest Hemingway in *The Greatest Hunting Stories Ever Told,* edited by Lamar Underwood, in 2000.

Although he hunted for sport, Roosevelt had a profound respect for nature. He said, "Encouragement of a proper hunting spirit, a proper love of sport, instead of being incompatible with a love of nature and wild things, offers the best guaranty for the preservation of wild things." His adoration for wildlife became the subject of public media when *Washington Post* cartoonist Clifford Berryman captured a sympathetic image of the president. A bit of revisionist history, *Drawing the Line in Mississippi* showed Roosevelt refusing to kill a bear cub when in fact what the cartoonist had witnessed in the autumn of 1902 was Roosevelt telling his hunting companions to humanely put down a wounded bear the dogs had cornered. In any event, according to the History Channel, the cartoon "depicted Roosevelt's dual accomplishments on the trip—negotiating border disputes and protecting wildlife."

Roosevelt's appreciation for nature had been instilled in him by his father. Having descended from Dutch settlers who gained riches as importers when they came to America in the 1640s, Theodore Roosevelt, Sr., had the means to pursue philanthropy. In fact, the original charter for the American Museum of Natural History was signed at the Roosevelt house when his son was around ten years old. "Just before my fourteenth birthday my father then a trustee of the American Museum of Natural History—started me on my rather mothlike career as a naturalist by giving me a pair of spectacles, a French pin-fire double-barreled shotgun—and lessons in stuffing birds," wrote Roosevelt in "My Life as a Naturalist" for *The American Museum Journal* in May 1918, demonstrating his dedication to the museum's vision to promote natural-history education. The museum, acknowledging his awareness of science, sent him on foreign expeditions and later commemorated his achievements by establishing a permanent exhibit, the Theodore Roosevelt Memorial Hall, which depicts Roosevelt's contributions to the study of natural history.

Roosevelt extended his hunting and museum philanthropy beyond the realm of hobby, actively recognizing the lasting importance of the United States' natural resources. While developing the

Panama Canal and mediating the Russo-Japanese War—for which he was awarded the Nobel Peace Prize—Roosevelt met with conservationists and altered the course of American history. Founding the Boone and Crockett Club in 1887, "His vision was to establish a coalition of dedicated conservationists and sportsmen who would provide the leadership needed to address the issues that affect hunting, wildlife and wild habitat," according to the Club. In 1903 Roosevelt went camping in Yosemite with John Muir, one of the founders of the Sierra Club, who greatly influenced Roosevelt's efforts to save America's breathtaking landscape. After being elected president in 1904, Roosevelt created the United States Forestry Service, which he turned over to conservationist Gifford Pinchot. According to the National Park Service, "During Roosevelt's time as President, the forest reserves in the U.S. went from approximately 43-million acres to about 194-million acres." Besides establishing 150 national forests, Roosevelt also established five national parks—Crater Lake, Oregon; Mesa Verde, Colorado; Platt, Oklahoma; Sullys Hill, North Dakota; Wind Cave, South Dakota—and fifty-one wildlife refuges.

After he left Washington, D.C., Roosevelt continued to be an influence in natural history. Roosevelt took Kermit (1889-1943), one of his six children with him on his post-presidential adventure travels to Africa and South America and attributed his son with saving his life. *The Happy Hunting-Grounds* is Kermit's recollections of going on safaris with his father and exploring on his own. His father once said of his son, "It is rare for a boy with his refined tastes and his genuine appreciation of literature—and of so much else—to be also an exceptionally bold and hardy sportsman." Kermit and his brother Theodore, Jr., inherited their father's interest in bears and the two co-wrote *Trailing the Great Panda*. Meanwhile, when Franklin D. Roosevelt became the nation's thirty-second president, he furthered his cousin's vision by signing the 1937 Federal Aid in Wildlife Restoration Act, which imposed on hunting guns a 10% tax that went to fund wildlife restoration. One of the nation's most beloved presidents, Theodore Roosevelt's connection to nature continues to be seen today: among the many things named after him are a national park and a species of elk.

Although Roosevelt does not have the distinction of being the first president to write a book—his predecessors include Thomas Jefferson, James Madison, and Ulysses S. Grant—he was the first president to ride in a car, fly in an airplane, and dive in a submarine, once again evidence of his adventurous spirit. His hunting literature is a lasting treasury of America's natural heritage and, combined with legislative action, it furthered the preservation of the United States' landscape, resources, and wildlife.

Stephanie Nikolopoulos is an editor at Barnes & Noble Books. Her writing has appeared in newspapers and magazines across the United States.

CHAPTER I

THE BISON OR AMERICAN BUFFALO

WHEN we became a nation, in 1776, the buffaloes, the first animals to vanish when the wilderness is settled, roved to the crests
of the mountains which mark the western boundaries of
Pennsylvania, Virginia, and the Carolinas. They were plentiful in
what are now the states of Ohio, Kentucky, and Tennessee. But by
the beginning of the present century they had been driven
beyond the Mississippi; and for the next eighty years they formed
one of the most distinctive and characteristic features of existence
on the great plains. Their numbers were countless—incredible. In
vast herds of hundreds of thousands of individuals, they roamed
from the Saskatchewan to the Rio Grande and westward to the
Rocky Mountains. They furnished all the means of livelihood to
the tribes of Horse Indians, and to the curious population of
French Metis, or Half-breeds, on the Red River, as well as to those
dauntless and archetypical wanderers, the white hunters and trappers. Their numbers slowly diminished, but the decrease was very
gradual until after the Civil War. They were not destroyed by the
settlers, but by the railways and the skin hunters.

After the ending of the Civil War, the work of constructing
trans-continental railway lines was pushed forward with the utmost
vigor. These supplied cheap and indispensable, but hitherto
wholly lacking, means of transportation to the hunters; and at the
same time the demand for buffalo robes and hides became very

great, while the enormous numbers of the beasts, and the comparative ease with which they were slaughtered, attracted throngs
of adventurers. The result was such a slaughter of big game as the
world had never before seen; never before were so many large
animals of one species destroyed in so short a time. Several million
buffaloes were slain. In fifteen years from the time the destruction
fairly began the great herds were exterminated. In all probability
there are not now, all told, five hundred head of wild buffaloes on
the American continent; and no herd of a hundred individuals
has been in existence since 1884.

The first great break followed the building of the Union Pacific
Railway. All the buffaloes of the middle region were then
destroyed, and the others were split into two vast sets of herds, the
northern and the southern. The latter were destroyed first, about
1878; the former not until 1883. My own chief experience with
buffaloes was obtained in the latter year, among small bands and
scattered individuals, near my ranch on the Little Missouri; I have
related it elsewhere. But two of my kinsmen were more fortunate
and took part in the chase of these lordly beasts when the herds
still darkened the prairie as far as the eye could see.

During the first two months of 1877, my brother Elliott, then a
lad not seventeen years old, made a buffalo-hunt toward the edge of
the Staked Plains in northern Texas. He was thus in at the death of
the southern herds; for all, save a few scattering bands, were
destroyed within two years of this time. He was with my cousin, John
Roosevelt, and they went out on the range with six other adventurers. It was a party of just such young men as frequently drift to the
frontier. All were short of cash, and all were hardy, vigorous fellows,
eager for excitement and adventure. My brother was much the
youngest of the party, and the least experienced; but he was well-
grown, strong and healthy, and very fond of boxing, wrestling,
running, riding, and shooting; moreover, he had served an appren-
ticeship in hunting deer and turkeys. Their mess-kit, ammunition,
bedding, and provisions were carried in two prairie-wagons, each
drawn by four horses. In addition to the teams they had six saddle-

animals—all of them shaggy, unkempt mustangs. Three or four dogs, setters and half-bred greyhounds, trotted along behind the wagons. Each man took his turn for two days as teamster and cook; and there were always two with the wagons, or camp, as the case might be, while the other six were off hunting, usually in couples. The expedition was undertaken partly for sport and partly with the hope of profit; for, after purchasing the horses and wagons, none of the party had any money left, and they were forced to rely upon selling skins and hides, and when near the forts, meat.

They started on January 2d, and shaped their course for the head-waters of the Salt Fork of the Brazos, the centre of abundance for the great buffalo herds. During the first few days they were in the outskirts of the settled country, and shot only small game—quail and prairie fowl; then they began to kill turkey, deer, and antelope. These they swapped for flour and feed at the ranches or squalid, straggling frontier towns. On several occasions the hunters were lost, spending the night out in the open, or sleeping at a ranch, if one was found. Both towns and ranches were filled with rough customers; all of my brother's companions were muscular, hotheaded fellows; and as a consequence they were involved in several savage free fights, in which, fortunately, nobody was seriously hurt. My brother kept a very brief diary, the entries being fairly startling from their conciseness. A number of times the mention of their arrival, either at a halting-place, a little village, or a rival buffalo camp, is followed by the laconic remark, "big fight," or "big row"; but once they evidently concluded discretion to be the better part of valor, the entry for January 20th being, "On the road—passed through Belknap—too lively, so kept on to the Brazos—very late." The buffalo-camps in particular were very jealous of one another, each party regarding itself as having exclusive right to the range it was the first to find; and on several occasions this feeling came near involving my brother and his companions in serious trouble.

While slowly driving the heavy wagons to the hunting grounds they suffered the usual hardships of plains travel. The weather, as in most Texas winters, alternated between the extremes of heat and cold. There had been little rain; in consequence water was scarce. Twice they were forced to cross wild, barren wastes, where the pools had dried up, and they suffered terribly from thirst. On the first occasion the horses were in good condition, and they traveled steadily, with only occasional short halts, for over thirty-six hours, by which time they were across the waterless country. The journal reads: "January 27th.—Big hunt—no water, and we left Quinn's blockhouse this morning 3 A.M.—on the go all night—hot. January 28.—No water—hot—at seven we struck water, and by eight Stinking Creek—grand 'hurrah.'" On the second occasion, the horses were weak and traveled slowly, so the party went forty-eight hours without drinking. "February 19th.—Pulled on twenty-one miles—trail bad—freezing night, no water, and wolves after our fresh meat. 20.—Made nineteen miles over prairie; again only mud, no water, freezing hard—frightful thirst. 21st.—Thirty miles to Clear Fork, fresh water." These entries were hurriedly jotted down at the time, by a boy who deemed it unmanly to make any especial note of hardship or suffering; but every plainsman will understand the real agony implied in working hard for two nights, one day, and portions of two others, without water, even in cool weather. During the last few miles the staggering horses were only just able to drag the lightly loaded wagon—for they had but one with them at the time—while the men plodded along in sullen silence, their mouths so parched that they could hardly utter a word. My own hunting and ranching were done in the North where there is more water; so I have never had a similar experience. Once I took a team in thirty-six hours across a country where there was no water; but by good luck it rained heavily in the night, so that the horses had plenty of wet grass, and I caught the rain in my slicker, and so had enough water for myself. Personally, I have but once been as long as twenty-six hours without water.

The party pitched their permanent camp in a canyon of the Brazos known as Canyon Blanco. The last few days of their journey they traveled beside the river through a veritable hunter's paradise. The drought had forced all the animals to come to the larger water-courses, and the country was literally swarming with game. Every day, and all day long, the wagons traveled through the herds of antelopes that grazed on every side, while, whenever they approached the canyon brink, bands of deer started from the timber that fringed the river's course; often, even the deer wandered out on the prairie with the antelope. Nor was the game shy; for the hunters, both red and white, followed only the buffaloes, until the huge, shaggy herds were destroyed, and the smaller beasts were in consequence but little molested.

Once my brother shot five antelopes from a single stand, when the party were short of fresh venison; he was out of sight and to leeward, and the antelopes seemed confused rather than alarmed at the rifle-reports and the fall of their companions. As was to be expected where game was so plenty, wolves and coyotes also abounded. At night they surrounded the camp, wailing and howling in a kind of shrieking chorus throughout the hours of darkness; one night they came up so close that the frightened horses had to be hobbled and guarded. On another occasion a large wolf actually crept into camp, where he was seized by the dogs, and the yelling, writhing knot of combatants rolled over one of the sleepers; finally, the long-toothed prowler managed to shake himself loose, and vanished in the gloom. One evening they were almost as much startled by a visit of a different kind. They were just finishing supper when an Indian stalked suddenly and silently out of the surrounding darkness, squatted down in the circle of firelight, remarked gravely, "Me Tonk," and began helping himself from the stew. He belonged to the friendly tribe of Tonkaways, so his hosts speedily recovered their equanimity; as for him, he had never lost his, and he sat eating by the fire until there was literally nothing left to eat. The panic caused by his appearance was natural; for at that time the Comanches were a scourge to the buffalo-hunters, ambushing them and raiding their camps; and several bloody fights had taken place.

Their camp had been pitched near a deep pool or water-hole. On both sides the bluffs rose like walls, and where they had crumbled and lost their sheerness, the vast buffalo herds, passing and repassing for countless generations, had worn furrowed trails so deep that the backs of the beasts were but little above the surrounding soil. In the bottom, and in places along the crests of the cliffs that hemmed in the canyon-like valley, there were groves of tangled trees, tenanted by great flocks of wild turkeys. Once my brother made two really remarkable shots at a pair of these great birds. It was at dusk, and they were flying directly overhead from one cliff to the other. He had in his hand a thirty-eight calibre Ballard rifle, and, as the gobblers winged their way heavily by, he brought both down with two successive bullets. This was of course mainly a piece of mere luck; but it meant good shooting, too. The Ballard was a very accurate, handy little weapon; it belonged to me, and was the first rifle I ever owned or used. With it I had once killed a deer, the only specimen of large game I had then shot; and I presented the rifle to my brother when he went to Texas. In our happy ignorance we deemed it quite good enough for buffalo or anything else; but out on the plains my brother soon found himself forced to procure a heavier and more deadly weapon.

When camp was pitched the horses were turned loose to graze and refresh themselves after their trying journey, during which they had lost flesh woefully. They were watched and tended by the two men who were always left in camp, and, save on rare occasions, were only used to haul in the buffalo hides. The camp-guards for the time being acted as cooks; and, though coffee and flour both ran short and finally gave out, fresh meat of every kind was abundant. The camp was never without buffalo-beef, deer, and antelope venison, wild turkeys, prairie-chickens, quails, ducks, and rabbits. The birds were simply "potted," as occasion required; when the quarry was deer or antelope, the hunters took the dogs with them to run down the wounded animals. But almost the entire attention of the hunters was given to the buffalo. After an evening spent in lounging round the camp-fire and a sound night's sleep, wrapped in robes and blankets, they would get up before daybreak, snatch a hurried breakfast, and start off in couples through the chilly dawn. The great beasts were very plentiful; in the first day's hunt twenty were slain; but the herds were restless and ever on the move. Sometimes they would be seen right by the camp, and again it would need an all-day's tramp to find them. There was no difficulty in spying them—the chief trouble with forest game; for on the prairie a buffalo makes no effort to hide and its black, shaggy bulk looms up as far as the eye can see. Sometimes they were found in small parties of three or four individuals, sometimes in bands of about two hundred, and again in great herds of many thousands; and solitary old bulls, expelled from the herds, were common. If on broken land, among hills and ravines, there was not much difficulty in approaching from the leeward; for, though the sense of smell in the buffalo is very acute, they do not see well at a distance through their overhanging frontlets of coarse and matted hair. If, as was generally the case, they were out on the open, rolling prairie, the stalking was far more difficult. Every hollow, every earth hummock and sagebush had to be used as cover. The hunter wriggled through the grass flat on his face, pushing himself along for perhaps a quarter of a mile by his toes and fingers, heedless of the spiny cactus. When near enough to the huge, unconscious quarry the hunter began firing, still keeping himself carefully concealed. If the smoke was blown away by the wind, and if the buffaloes caught no glimpse of the assailant, they would often stand motionless and stupid until many of their number had been slain, the hunter being careful not to fire too high, aiming just behind the shoulder, about a third of the way up the body, that his bullet might go through the lungs. Sometimes, even after they saw the man, they would act as if confused and panic-struck, huddling together and staring at the smoke puffs; but generally they were off at a lumbering gallop as soon as they had an idea of the point of danger. When once started, they ran for many miles before halting, and their pursuit on foot was extremely laborious.

One morning my cousin and brother had been left in camp as guards. They were sitting idly warming themselves in the first sunbeams, when their attention was sharply drawn to four buffaloes that were coming to the pool to drink. The beasts came down a game trail, a deep rut in the bluff, fronting where they were sitting, and they did not dare to stir for fear of being discovered. The buffaloes walked into the pool, and after drinking their fill, stood for some time with the water running out of their mouths, idly lashing their sides with their short tails, enjoying the bright warmth of the early sunshine; then, with much splashing and the gurgling of soft mud, they left the pool and clambered up the bluff with unwieldy agility. As soon as they turned, my brother and cousin ran for their rifles, but before they got back the buffaloes had crossed the bluff crest. Climbing after them, the two hunters found, when they reached the summit, that their game, instead of halting, had struck straight off across the prairie at a slow lope, doubtless intending to rejoin the herd they had left. After a moment's consultation the men went in pursuit, excitement overcoming their knowledge that they ought not, by rights, to leave camp. They struck a steady trot, following the animals by sight until they passed over a knoll, and then trailing them. Where the grass was long, as it was for the first four or five miles, this was a work of no difficulty, and they did not break their gait, only glancing now and then at the trail. As the sun rose and the day became warm, their breathing grew quicker; and the sweat rolled off their faces as they ran across the rough prairie sward, up and down the long inclines, now and then shifting their heavy rifles from one shoulder to the other. But they were in good training, and they did not have to halt. At last they reached stretches of bare ground, sun-baked and grassless, where the trail grew dim; and here they had to go very slowly, carefully examining the faint dents and marks made in the soil by the heavy hoofs, and unraveling the trail from the mass of old footmarks. It was tedious work, but it enabled them to completely recover their breath by the time that they again struck the grassland; and but a few hundred yards from its edge, in a slight hollow, they saw the four buffaloes just entering a herd of fifty or sixty that were scattered out grazing. The herd paid no attention to the newcomers, and these immediately began to feed greedily. After a whispered consultation, the two hunters crept back, and made a long circle that brought them well to leeward of the herd, in line with a slight rise in the ground. They then crawled up to this rise and, peering through the tufts of tall, rank grass, saw the unconscious beasts a hundred and twenty-five or fifty yards away. They fired together, each mortally wounding his animal, and then, rushing in as the herd halted in confusion, and following them as they ran, impeded by numbers, hurry, and panic, they eventually got three more.

On another occasion the same two hunters nearly met with a frightful death, being overtaken by a vast herd of stampeded buffaloes. All animals that go in herds are subject to these instantaneous attacks of uncontrollable terror, under the influence of which they become perfectly mad, and rush headlong in dense masses on any form of death. Horses, and more especially cattle, often suffer from stampedes; it is a danger against which the cowboys are compelled to be perpetually on guard. A band of stampeded horses, sweeping in mad terror up a valley, will dash against a rock or tree with such violence as to leave several dead animals at its base, while the survivors race on without halting; they will overturn and destroy tents and wagons, and a man on foot caught in the rush has but a small chance for his life. A buffalo stampede is much worse—or rather was much worse, in the old days—because of the great weight and immense numbers of the beasts, which, in a fury of heedless terror, plunged over cliffs and into rivers, and bore down whatever was in their path. On the occasion in question, my brother and cousin were on their way homeward. They were just mounting one of the long, low swells, into which the prairie was broken, when they heard a low, muttering, rumbling noise, like far-off thunder. It grew steadily louder, and, not knowing what it meant, they hurried forward to the top of the rise. As they reached it, they stopped short in terror and amazement, for before them the whole prairie was black with madly rushing buffaloes.

Afterward they learned that another couple of hunters, four or five miles off, had fired into and stampeded a large herd. This herd, in its rush, gathered others, all thundering along together in uncontrollable and increasing panic.

The surprised hunters were far away from any broken ground or other place of refuge, while the vast herd of huge, plunging, maddened beasts was charging straight down on them not a quarter of a mile distant. Down they came! — thousands upon thousands, their front extending a mile in breadth, while the earth shook beneath their thunderous gallop, and, as they came closer, their shaggy frontlets loomed dimly through the columns of dust thrown up from the dry soil. The two hunters knew that their only hope for life was to split the herd, which, though it had so broad a front, was not very deep. If they failed they would inevitably be trampled to death.

Waiting until the beasts were in close range, they opened a rapid fire from their heavy breech-loading rifles, yelling at the top of their voices. For a moment the result seemed doubtful. The line thundered steadily down on them; then it swayed violently, as two or three of the brutes immediately in their front fell beneath the bullets, while their neighbors made violent efforts to press off sidewise. Then a narrow wedge-shaped rift appeared in the line, widening as it came closer, and the buffaloes, shrinking from their foes in front, strove desperately to edge away from the dangerous neighborhood: shouts and shots were redoubled; the hunters were almost choked by the cloud of dust, through which they could see the stream of dark huge bodies passing within rifle-length on either side; and in a moment the peril was over, and the two men were left alone on the plain, unharmed, though with their nerves terribly shaken. The herd careered on toward the horizon, save five individuals which had been killed or disabled by the shots.

On another occasion, when my brother was out with one of his friends, they fired at a small herd containing an old bull; the bull charged the smoke, and the whole herd followed him.

Probably they were simply stampeded, and had no hostile intention; at any rate, after the death of their leader, they rushed by without doing any damage.

But buffaloes sometimes charged with the utmost determination, and were then dangerous antagonists. My cousin, a very hardy and resolute hunter, had a narrow escape from a wounded cow which he followed up a steep bluff or sand cliff. Just as he reached the summit, he was charged, and was only saved by the sudden appearance of his dog, which distracted the cow's attention. He thus escaped with only a tumble and a few bruises.

My brother also came in for a charge, while killing the biggest bull that was slain by any of the party. He was out alone, and saw a small herd of cows and calves at some distance, with a huge bull among them, towering above them like a giant. There was no break in the ground, nor any tree nor bush near them, but, by making a half-circle, my brother managed to creep up against the wind behind a slight roll in the prairie surface, until he was within seventy-five yards of the grazing and unconscious beasts. There were some cows and calves between him and the bull, and he had to wait some moments before they shifted position, as the herd grazed onward and gave him a fair shot; in the interval they had moved so far forward that he was in plain view. His first bullet struck just behind the shoulder; the herd started and looked around, but the bull merely lifted his head and took a step forward, his tail curled up over his back. The next bullet likewise struck fair, nearly in the same place, telling with a loud "pack!" against the thick hide, and making the dust fly up from the matted hair. Instantly the great bull wheeled and charged in headlong anger, while the herd fled in the opposite direction. On the bare prairie, with no spot of refuge, it was useless to try to escape, and the hunter, with reloaded rifle, waited until the bull was not far off, then drew up his weapon and fired. Either he was nervous, or the bull at the moment bounded over some obstacle, for the ball went a little wild; nevertheless, by good luck, it broke a fore-leg, and the great beast came crashing to the earth, and was slain before it could struggle to its feet.

Two days after this event, a war party of Comanches swept down along the river. They "jumped" a neighboring camp, killing one man and wounding two more, and at the same time ran off all but three of the horses belonging to our eight adventurers. With the remaining three horses and one wagon they set out homeward. The march was hard and tedious; they lost their way and were in jeopardy from quicksands and cloudbursts; they suffered from thirst and cold, their shoes gave out, and their feet were lamed by cactus spines. At last they reached Fort Griffen in safety, and great was their ravenous rejoicing when they procured some bread—for during the final fortnight of the hunt they had been without flour or vegetables of any kind, or even coffee, and had subsisted on fresh meat "straight." Nevertheless, it was a very healthy, as well as a very pleasant and exciting experience; and I doubt if any of those who took part in it will ever forget their great buffalo-hunt on the Brazos.

My friend, General W. H. Walker of Virginia, had an experience in the early '50s with buffaloes on the upper Arkansas River, which gives some idea of their enormous numbers at that time. He was camped with a scouting party on the banks of the river, and had gone out to try to shoot some meat. There were many buffaloes in sight, scattered, according to their custom, in large bands. When he was a mile or two away from the river a dull roaring sound in the distance attracted his attention, and he saw that a herd of buffalo far to the south, away from the river, had been stampeded and was running his way. He knew that if he was caught in the open by the stampeded herd his chance for life would be small, and at once ran for the river. By desperate efforts he reached the breaks in the sheer banks just as the buffaloes reached them, and got into a position of safety on the pinnacle of a little bluff. From this point of vantage he could see the entire plain. To the very verge of the horizon the brown masses of the buffalo bands showed through the dust clouds, coming on with a thunderous roar like that of surf. Camp was a mile away, and the stampede luckily passed to one side of it. Watching his chance he finally dodged back to the tent, and all that afternoon watched the immense masses of buffalo, as band after band tore to the brink of the bluffs on one side, raced down them, rushed through the water, up the bluffs on the other side, and again off over the plain, churning the sandy, shallow stream into a ceaseless tumult. When darkness fell there was no apparent decrease in the numbers that were passing, and all through that night the continuous roar showed that the herds were still threshing across the river. Toward dawn the sound at last ceased, and General Walker arose somewhat irritated, as he had reckoned on killing an ample supply of meat, and he supposed that there would be now no bison left south of the river. To his astonishment, when he strolled up on the bluffs and looked over the plain, it was still covered far and wide with groups of buffalo, grazing quietly. Apparently there were as many on that side as ever, in spite of the many scores of thousands that must have crossed over the river during the stampede of the afternoon and night. The barren-ground caribou is the only American animal which is now ever seen in such enormous herds.

In 1862 Mr. Clarence King, while riding along the overland trail through western Kansas, passed through a great buffalo herd, and was himself injured in an encounter with a bull. The great herd was then passing north, and Mr. King reckoned that it must have covered an area nearly seventy miles by thirty in extent; the figures representing his rough guess, made after traveling through the herd crosswise, and upon knowing how long it took to pass a given point going northward. This great herd of course was not a solid mass of buffaloes; it consisted of innumerable bands of every size, dotting the prairie within the limits given. Mr. King was mounted on a somewhat unmanageable horse. On one occasion in following a band he wounded a large bull, and became so wedged in by the maddened animals that he was unable to avoid the charge of the bull, which was at its last gasp. Coming straight toward him it leaped into the air and struck the afterpart of the saddle full with its massive forehead. The horse was hurled to the ground with a broken back, and King's leg was likewise broken, while the bull turned a complete somerset over them and never rose again.

In the recesses of the Rocky Mountains, from Colorado northward through Alberta, and in the depths of the subarctic forest beyond the Saskatchewan, there have always been found small numbers of the bison, locally called the mountain buffalo and wood buffalo; often indeed the old hunters term these animals "bison," although they never speak of the plains animals save as buffalo. They form a slight variety of what was formerly the ordinary plains bison, intergrading with it; on the whole they are darker in color, with longer, thicker hair, and in consequence with the appearance of being heavier-bodied and shorter-legged. They have been sometimes spoken of as forming a separate species; but, judging from my own limited experience, and from a comparison of the many hides I have seen, I think they are really the same animal, many individuals of the two so-called varieties being quite indistinguishable. In fact the only moderate-sized herd of wild bison in existence to-day, the protected herd in the Yellowstone Park, is composed of animals intermediate in habits and coat between the mountain and plains varieties — as were all the herds of the Bighorn, Big Hole, Upper Madison, and Upper Yellowstone valleys.

However, the habitat of these wood and mountain bison yielded them shelter from hunters in a way that the plains never could, and hence they have always been harder to kill in the one place than in the other; for precisely the same reasons that have held good with the elk, which have been completely exterminated from the plains, while still abundant in many of the forest fastnesses of the Rockies. Moreover, the bison's dull eyesight is no special harm in the woods, while it is peculiarly hurtful to the safety of any beast on the plains, where eyesight avails more than any other sense, the true game of the plains being the prong-buck, the most keen-sighted of American animals. On the other hand, the bison's hearing, of little avail on the plains, is of much assistance in the woods; and its excellent nose helps equally in both places.

Though it was always more difficult to kill the bison of the forests and mountains than the bison of the prairie, yet now that the species is, in its wild state, hovering on the brink of extinction, the difficulty is immeasurably increased. A merciless and terrible process of natural selection, in which the agents were rifle-bearing hunters, has left as the last survivors in a hopeless struggle for existence only the wariest of the bison and those gifted with the sharpest senses. That this was true of the last lingering individuals that survived the great slaughter on the plains is well shown by Mr. Hornaday in his graphic account of his campaign against the few scattered buffalo which still lived in 1886 between the Missouri and the Yellowstone, along the Big Dry. The bison of the plains and the prairies have now vanished; and so few of their brethren of the mountains and the northern forests are left, that they can just barely be reckoned among American game; but whoever is so fortunate as to find any of these animals must work his hardest, and show all his skill as a hunter if he wishes to get one.

In the fall of 1889 I heard that a very few bison were still left around the head of Wisdom River. Thither I went and hunted faithfully; there was plenty of game of other kind, but of bison not a trace did we see. Nevertheless a few days later that same year I came across these great wild cattle at a time when I had no idea of seeing them.

It was, as nearly as we could tell, in Idaho, just south of the Montana boundary line, and some twenty-five miles west of the line of Wyoming. We were camped high among the mountains, with a small pack-train. On the day in question we had gone out to find moose, but had seen no sign of them, and had then begun to climb over the higher peaks with an idea of getting sheep. The old hunter who was with me was, very fortunately, suffering from rheumatism, and he therefore carried a long staff instead of his rifle; I say fortunately, for if he had carried his rifle it would have been impossible to stop his firing at such game as bison, nor would he have spared the cows and calves.

About the middle of the afternoon we crossed a low, rocky ridge, above timber line, and saw at our feet a basin or round valley of singular beauty. Its walls were formed by steep mountains. At its upper end lay a small lake, bordered on one side by a meadow of emerald green. The lake's other side marked the edge of the frowning pine forest which filled the rest of the valley, and hung high on the sides of the gorge which formed its outlet. Beyond the lake the ground rose in a pass evidently much frequented by game in bygone days, their trails lying along it in thick zigzags, each gradually fading out after a few hundred yards, and then starting again in a little different place, as game trails so often seem to do.

We bent our steps toward these trails, and no sooner had we reached the first than the old hunter bent over it with a sharp exclamation of wonder. There in the dust were the unmistakable hoof-marks of a small band of bison, apparently but a few hours old. They were headed toward the lake. There had been half a dozen animals in the party; one a big bull, and two calves.

We immediately turned and followed the trail. It led down to the little lake, where the beasts had spread and grazed on the tender, green blades, and had drunk their fill. The footprints then came together again, showing where the animals had gathered and walked off in single file to the forest. Evidently they had come to the pool in the early morning, walking over the game pass from some neighboring valley, and after drinking and feeding had moved into the pine forest to find some spot for their noontide rest.

It was a very still day, and there were nearly three hours of daylight left. Without a word my silent companion, who had been scanning the whole country with hawk-eyed eagerness, besides scrutinizing the sign on his hands and knees, took the trail, motioning me to follow. In a moment we entered the woods, breathing a sigh of relief as we did so; for while in the meadow we could never tell that the buffalo might not see us, if they happened to be lying in some place with a commanding lookout.

The old hunter was thoroughly roused, and he showed himself a very skilful tracker. We were much favored by the character of the forest, which was rather open, and in most places free from undergrowth and down timber. As in most Rocky Mountain forests the timber was small, not only as compared to the giant trees of the groves of the Pacific Coast, but as compared to the forests of the Northeast. The ground was covered with pine needles and soft moss, so that it was not difficult to walk noiselessly. Once or twice when I trod on a small dry twig, or let the nails in my shoes clink slightly against a stone, the hunter turned to me with a frown of angry impatience; but as he walked slowly, continually halting to look ahead, as well as stooping over to examine the trail, I did not find it very difficult to move silently. I kept a little behind him and to one side, save when he crouched to take advantage of some piece of cover, and I crept in his footsteps. I did not look at the trail at all, but kept watching ahead, hoping at any moment to see the game.

It was not very long before we struck their day beds, which were made on a knoll, where the forest was open and where there was much down timber. After leaving the day beds the animals had at first fed separately around the grassy base and sides of the knoll, and had then made off in their usual single file, going straight to a small pool in the forest. After drinking they had left this pool, and traveled down toward the gorge at the mouth of the basin, the trail leading along the sides of the steep hill, which were dotted by open glades; while the roar of the cataracts by which the stream was broken ascended from below. Here we moved with redoubled caution, for the sign had grown very fresh and the animals had once more scattered and begun feeding. When the trail led across the glades we usually skirted them so as to keep in the timber.

At last, on nearing the edge of one of these glades we saw a movement among the young trees on the other side, not fifty yards away. Peering through the safe shelter yielded by some thick evergreen bushes, we speedily made out three bison, a cow, a calf, and a yearling, grazing greedily on the other side of the glade, under the fringing timber; all with their heads up hill. Soon another cow and calf stepped out after them. I did not wish to shoot, waiting for the appearance of the big bull which I knew was accompanying them.

So for several minutes I watched the great, clumsy, shaggy beasts, as all unconscious they grazed in the open glade. Behind them rose the dark pines. At the left of the glade the ground fell away to form the side of a chasm; down in its depths the cataracts foamed and thundered; beyond, the huge mountains towered, their crests crimsoned by the sinking sun. Mixed with the eager excitement of the hunter was a certain half melancholy feeling as I gazed on these bison, themselves part of the last remnant of a doomed and nearly vanished race. Few, indeed, are the men who now have, or ever more shall have, the chance of seeing the mightiest of American beasts, in all his wild vigor, surrounded by the tremendous desolation of his far-off mountain home.

At last, when I had begun to grow very anxious lest the others should take alarm, the bull likewise appeared on the edge of the glade, and stood with outstretched head, scratching his throat against a young tree, which shook violently. I aimed low, behind his shoulder, and pulled trigger. At the crack of the rifle all the bison, without the momentary halt of terror-struck surprise so common among game, turned and raced off at headlong speed. The fringe of young pines beyond and below the glade cracked and swayed as if a whirlwind were passing, and in another moment they reached the top of a very steep incline, thickly strewn with boulders and dead timber. Down this they plunged with reckless speed; their surefootedness was a marvel in such seemingly unwieldy beasts. A column of dust obscured their passage, and under its cover they disappeared in the forest; but the trail of the bull was marked by splashes of frothy blood, and we followed it at a trot. Fifty yards beyond the border of the forest we found the stark black body stretched motionless. He was a splendid old bull, still in his full vigor, with large, sharp horns, and heavy mane and glossy coat; and I felt the most exulting pride as I handled and examined him; for I had procured a trophy such as can fall henceforth to few hunters indeed.

It was too late to dress the beast that evening; so, after taking out the tongue and cutting off enough meat for supper and breakfast, we scrambled down to near the torrent, and after some search found a good spot for camping. Hot and dusty from the day's hard tramp, I undressed and took a plunge in the stream, the icy water making me gasp. Then, having built a slight lean-to of brush, and dragged together enough dead timber to burn all night, we cut long alder twigs, sat down before some embers raked apart, and grilled and ate our buffalo meat with the utmost relish. Night had fallen; a cold wind blew up the valley; the torrent roared as it leaped past us, and drowned our words as we strove to talk over our adventures and success; while the flame of the fire flickered and danced, lighting up with continual vivid flashes the gloom of the forest round about.

CHAPTER II

THE BLACK BEAR

NEXT to the whitetail deer the black bear is the commonest and most widely distributed of American big game. It is still found quite plentifully in northern New England, in the Adirondacks, Catskills, and along the entire length of the Alleghanies, as well as in the swamps and canebrakes of the Southern States. It is also common in the great forests of northern Michigan, Wisconsin, and Minnesota, and throughout the Rocky Mountains and the timbered ranges of the Pacific Coast. In the East it has always ranked second only to the deer among the beasts of chase. The bear and the buck were the staple objects of pursuit of all the old hunters. They were more plentiful than the bison and elk even in the long vanished days when these two great monarchs of the forest still ranged eastward to Virginia and Pennsylvania. The wolf and the cougar were always too scarce and too shy to yield much profit to the hunter. The black bear is a timid, cowardly animal, and usually a vegetarian, though it sometimes preys on the sheep, hogs, and even cattle of the settler, and is very fond of raiding his corn and melons. Its meat is good and its fur often valuable; and in its chase there is much excitement, and occasionally a slight spice of danger, just enough to render it attractive; so it has always been eagerly followed. Yet it still holds its own, though in greatly diminished numbers, in the more thinly settled portions of the country. One of the standing riddles of American zoology is the fact that the black bear, which is easier killed and less prolific than the wolf, should hold its own in the land better than the latter, this being directly the reverse of what occurs in Europe, where the brown bear is generally exterminated before the wolf.

In a few wild spots in the East, in northern Maine, for instance, here and there in the neighborhood of the upper Great Lakes, in the east Tennessee and Kentucky mountains and the swamps of Florida and Mississippi, there still lingers an occasional representative of the old wilderness hunters. These men live in log-cabins in the wilderness. They do their hunting on foot, occasionally with the help of a single trailing dog. In Maine they are as apt to kill moose and caribou as bear and deer; but elsewhere the two last, with an occasional cougar or wolf, are the beasts of chase which they follow. Nowadays as these old hunters die there is no one to take their places, though there are still plenty of backwoods settlers in all of the regions named who do a great deal of hunting and trapping. Such an old hunter rarely makes his appearance at the settlements except to dispose of his peltry and hides in exchange for cartridges and provisions, and he leads a life of such lonely isolation as to ensure his individual characteristics developing into peculiarities. Most of the wilder districts in the Eastern States still preserve memories of some such old hunter who lived his long life alone, waging ceaseless warfare on the vanishing game, whose oddities, as well as his courage, hardihood, and woodcraft, are laughingly remembered by the older settlers, and who is usually best known as having killed the last wolf or bear or cougar ever seen in the locality.

Generally the weapon mainly relied on by these old hunters is the rifle; and occasionally some old hunter will be found even to this day who uses a muzzle-loader, such as Kit Carson carried in the middle of the century. There are exceptions to this rule of the rifle, however. In the years after the Civil War one of the many noted hunters of southwest Virginia and east Tennessee was Wilber Waters, sometimes called The Hunter of White Top. He often killed black bear with a knife and dogs. He spent all his life in hunting and was very successful, killing the last gang of wolves to be found in his neighborhood; and he slew innumerable bears, with no worse results to himself than an occasional bite or scratch.

In the southern States the planters living in the wilder regions have always been in the habit of following the black bear with horse and hound, many of them keeping regular packs of bear hounds. Such a pack includes not only pure-bred hounds, but also cross-bred animals, and some sharp, agile, hard-biting fierce dogs and terriers. They follow the bear and bring him to bay but do not try to kill him, although there are dogs of the big fighting breeds which can readily master a black bear if loosed at him three or four at a time; but the dogs of these Southern bear-hound packs are not fitted for such work, and if they try to close with the bear he is certain to play havoc with them, disemboweling them with blows of his paws or seizing them in his arms and biting through their spines or legs. The riders follow the hounds through the canebrakes, and also try to make cutoffs and station themselves at open points where they think the bear will pass, so that they may get a shot at him. The weapons used are rifles, shotguns, and occasionally revolvers.

Sometimes, however, the hunter uses the knife. General Wade Hampton, who has probably killed more black bears than any other man living in the United States, frequently used the knife, slaying thirty or forty with this weapon. His plan was, when he found that the dogs had the bear at bay, to walk up close and cheer them on. They would instantly seize the bear in a body, and he would then rush in and stab it behind the shoulder, reaching over so as to inflict the wound on the opposite side from that where he stood. He escaped scathless from all these encounters save one, in which he was rather severely torn in the forearm. Many other hunters have used the knife, but perhaps none so frequently as he; for he was always fond of steel, as witness his feats with the "white arm" during the Civil War.

General Hampton always hunted with large packs of hounds, managed sometimes by himself and sometimes by his negro hunters. He occasionally took out forty dogs at a time. He found that all his dogs together could not kill a big fat bear, but they occasionally killed three-year-olds, or lean and poor bears. During the course of his life he has himself killed or been in at the death of, five hundred bears, at least two-thirds of them falling by his own hand. In the year just before the war he had on one occasion, in Mississippi, killed sixty-eight bears in five months. Once he killed four bears in a day; at another time three, and frequently two. The two largest bears he himself killed weighed, respectively, 408 and 410 pounds. They were both shot in Mississippi. But he saw at least one bear killed which was much larger than either of these. These figures were taken down at the time, when the animals were actually weighed on the scales. Most of his hunting for bear was done in northern Mississippi, where one of his plantations was situated, near Greenville. During the half century that he hunted, on and off, in this neighborhood, he knew of two instances where hunters were fatally wounded in the chase of the black bear. Both of the men were inexperienced, one being a raftsman who came down the river, and the other a man from Vicksburg. He was not able to learn the particulars in the last case, but the raftsman came too close to a bear that was at bay, and it broke through the dogs, rushed at and overthrew him, then lying on him, it bit him deeply in the thigh, through the femoral artery, so that he speedily bled to death.

But a black bear is not usually a formidable opponent, and though he will sometimes charge home he is much more apt to bluster and bully than actually to come to close quarters. I myself have but once seen a man who had been hurt by one of these bears. This was an Indian. He had come on the beast close up in a thick wood, and had mortally wounded it with his gun; it had then closed with him, knocking the gun out of his hand, so that he was forced to use his knife. It charged him on all fours, but in the grapple, when it had failed to throw him down, it raised itself on its hind legs, clasping him across the shoulders with its fore-paws. Apparently it had no intention of hugging, but merely sought to draw him within reach of its jaws. He fought desperately against this, using the knife freely, and striving to keep its head back; and the flow of blood weakened the animal, so that it finally fell exhausted, before being able dangerously to injure him. But it had bitten his left arm very severely, and its claws had made long gashes on his shoulders.

Black bears, like grislies, vary greatly in their modes of attack. Sometimes they rush in and bite; and again they strike with their fore-paws. Two of my cowboys were originally from Maine, where I knew them well. There they were fond of trapping bears, and caught a good many. The huge steel gins, attached by chains to heavy clogs, prevented the trapped beasts from going far; and when found they were always tied tight round some tree or bush, and usually nearly exhausted. The men killed them either with a little 32-calibre pistol or a hatchet. But once did they meet with any difficulty. On this occasion one of them incautiously approached a captured bear to knock it on the head with his hatchet, but the animal managed to partially untwist itself, and with its free forearm made a rapid sweep at him; he jumped back just in time, the bear's claws tearing his clothes—after which he shot it. Bears are shy and have very keen noses; they are therefore hard to kill by fair hunting, living, as they generally do, in dense forests or thick brush. They are easy enough to trap, however. Thus, these two men, though they trapped so many, never but once killed them in any other way. On this occasion one of them, in the winter, found in a great hollow log a den where a she and two well-grown cubs had taken up their abode, and shot all three with his rifle as they burst out.

Where they are much hunted, bear become purely nocturnal; but in the wilder forests I have seen them abroad at all hours, though they do not much relish the intense heat of noon. They are rather comical animals to watch feeding and going about the ordinary business of their lives. Once I spent half an hour lying at the edge of a wood and looking at a black bear some three hundred yards off across an open glade. It was in good stalking country, but the wind was unfavorable and I waited for it to shift— waited too long as it proved, for something frightened the beast and he made off before I could get a shot at him. When I first saw him he was shuffling along and rooting in the ground, so that he looked like a great pig. Then he began to turn over the stones and logs to hunt for insects, small reptiles, and the like. A moderate-sized stone he would turn over with a single clap of his paw, and then plunge his nose down into the hollow to gobble up the small creatures beneath while still dazed by the light. The big logs and rocks he would tug and worry at with both paws; once, overexerting his clumsy strength, he lost his grip and rolled clean on his back. Under some of the logs he evidently found mice and chipmunks; then, as soon as the log was overturned, he would be seen jumping about with grotesque agility, and making quick dabs here and there, as the little scurrying rodent turned and twisted, until at last he put his paw on it and scooped it up into his mouth. Sometimes, probably when he smelt the mice underneath, he would cautiously turn the log over with one paw, holding the other lifted and ready to strike. Now and then he would halt and sniff the air in every direction, and it was after one of these halts that he suddenly shuffled off into the woods.

Black bear generally feed on berries, nuts, insects, carrion, and the like; but at times they take to killing very large animals. In fact, they are curiously irregular in their food. They will kill deer if they can get at them; but generally the deer are too quick. Sheep and hogs are their favorite prey, especially the latter, for bears seem to have a special relish for pork. Twice I have known a black bear kill cattle. Once the victim was a bull which had got mired, and which the bear deliberately proceeded to eat alive, heedless of the bellows of the unfortunate beast. On the other occasion, a cow was surprised and slain among some bushes at the edge of a remote pasture. In the spring, soon after the long winter sleep, they are very hungry, and are especially apt to attack large beasts at this time; although during the very first days of their appearance, when they are just breaking their fast, they eat rather sparingly, and by preference the tender shoots of green grass and other herbs, or frogs and crayfish; it is not for a week or two that they seem to be overcome by lean, ravenous hunger. They will even attack and master that formidable fighter the moose, springing at it from an ambush as it passes—for a bull moose would surely be an overmatch for one of them if fronted fairly in the open. An old hunter, whom I could trust, told me that he had seen in the snow in early spring the place where a bear had sprung at two moose, which were trotting together; he missed his spring, and the moose got off, their strides after they settled down into their pace being tremendous, and showing how thoroughly they were frightened. Another time he saw a bear chase a moose into a lake, where it waded out a little distance, and then turned to bay, bidding defiance to his pursuer, the latter not daring to approach in the water. I have been told—but can not vouch for it—that instances have been known where the bear, maddened by hunger, has gone in on a moose thus standing at bay, only to be beaten down under the water by the terrible fore-hoofs of the quarry, and to yield its life in the contest. A lumberman told me that he once saw a moose, evidently much startled, trot through a swamp, and immediately afterward a bear came up following the tracks. He almost ran into the man, and was evidently not in good temper, for he growled and blustered, and two or three times made feints of charging, before he finally concluded to go off.

Bears will occasionally visit hunters' or lumbermen's camps, in the absence of the owners, and play sad havoc with all that therein is, devouring everything eatable, especially if sweet, and trampling into a dirty mess whatever they do not eat. The black bear does not average more than a third the size of the grisly; but, like all its kind, it varies greatly in weight. The largest I myself ever saw weighed was in Maine, and tipped the scale at 346 pounds; but I have a perfectly authentic record of one in Maine that weighed 397, and my friend, Dr. Hart Merriam, tells me that he has seen several in the Adirondacks that when killed weighed about 350.

I have myself shot but one or two black bears, and these were obtained under circumstances of no especial interest, as I merely stumbled on them while after other game, and killed them before they had a chance either to run or show fight.

CHAPTER III

OLD EPHRAIM, THE GRISLY BEAR

THE king of the game beasts of temperate North America, because the most dangerous to the hunter, is the grisly bear; known to the few remaining old-time trappers of the Rockies and the Great Plains, sometimes as "Old Ephraim" and sometimes as "Moccasin Joe" — the last in allusion to his queer, half-human footprints, which look as if made by some misshapen giant, walking in moccasins.

Bear vary greatly in size and color, no less than in temper and habits. Old hunters speak much of them in their endless talks over the camp fires and in the snow-bound winter huts. They insist on many species; not merely the black and the grisly, but the brown, the cinnamon, the gray, the silver-tip, and others with names known only in certain localities, such as the range bear, the roach-back, and the smut-face. But, in spite of popular opinion to the contrary, most old hunters are very untrustworthy in dealing with points of natural history. They usually know only so much about any given game animal as will enable them to kill it. They study its habits solely with this end in view; and once slain they only examine it to see about its condition and fur. With rare exceptions they are quite incapable of passing judgment upon questions of specific identity or difference. When questioned, they not only advance perfectly impossible theories and facts in support of their views, but they rarely even agree as to the views themselves. One hunter will assert that the true grisly is only found in California, heedless of the fact that the name was first used by Lewis and Clark as one of the titles they applied to the large bears of the plains country round the Upper Missouri, a quarter of a century before the California grisly was known to fame. Another hunter will call any big brindled bear a grisly no matter where it is found; and he and his companions will dispute by the hour as to whether a bear of large, but not extreme, size is a grisly or a silver-tip. In Oregon the cinnamon bear is a phase of the small black bear; in Montana it is the plains variety of the large mountain silver-tip. I have myself seen the skins of two bears killed on the upper waters of Tongue River; one was that of a male, one of a female, and they had evidently just mated; yet one was distinctly a "silver-tip" and the other a "cinnamon." The skin of one very big bear which I killed in the Bighorn has proved a standing puzzle to almost all the old hunters to whom I have showed it; rarely do any two of them agree as to whether it is a grisly, a silver-tip, a cinnamon, or a "smut-face." Any bear with unusually long hair on the spine and shoulders, especially if killed in the spring, when the fur is shaggy, is forthwith dubbed a "roach-back." The average sporting writer moreover joins with the more imaginative members of the "old hunter" variety in ascribing wildly various traits to these different bears. One comments on the superior prowess of the roach-back; the explanation being that a bear in early spring is apt to be ravenous from hunger. The next insists that the California grisly is the only really dangerous bear; while another stoutly maintains that it does not compare in ferocity with what he calls the "smaller" silver-tip or cinnamon. And so on, and so on, without end. All of which is mere nonsense.

Nevertheless, it is no easy task to determine how many species or varieties of bear actually do exist in the United States, and I can not even say without doubt that a very large set of skins and skulls would not show a nearly complete intergradation between the most widely separated individuals. However, there are certainly two very distinct types, which differ almost as widely from each other as a wapiti does from a mule deer, and which exist in the same localities in most heavily timbered portions of the Rockies. One is the small black bear, a bear which will average about two hundred pounds' weight, with fine, glossy, black fur, and the fore-claws but little longer than the hinder ones; in fact the hairs of the fore-paw often reach to their tips. This bear is a tree-climber. It is the only kind found east of the great plains, and it is also plentiful in the forest-clad portions of the Rockies, being common in most heavily timbered tracts throughout the United States. The other is the grisly, which weighs three or four times as much as the black, and has a pelt of coarse hair, which is in color gray, grizzled, or brown of various shades. It is not a tree-climber, and the fore-claws are very long, much longer than the hinder ones. It is found from the great plains west of the Mississippi to the Pacific Coast. This bear inhabits indifferently the lowland and mountain; the deep woods, and the barren plains where the only cover is the stunted growth fringing the streams. These two types are very distinct in every way, and their differences are not at all dependent upon mere geographical considerations; for they are often found in the same district. Thus I found them both in the Bighorn Mountains, each type being in extreme form, while the specimens I shot showed no trace of intergradation. The huge grizzled, long-clawed beast, and its little glossy-coated, short-clawed, tree-climbing brother roamed over exactly the same country in those mountains; but they were as distinct in habits, and mixed as little together as moose and caribou.

On the other hand, when a sufficient number of bears, from widely separated regions, are examined, the various distinguishing marks are found to be inconstant and to show a tendency— exactly how strong I cannot say—to fade into one another. The differentiation of the two species seems to be as yet scarcely completed; there are more or less imperfect connecting links, and as regards the grisly it almost seems as if the specific characters were still unstable. In the far Northwest, in the basin of the Columbia, the "black" bear is as often brown as any other color; and I have seen the skins of two cubs, one black and one brown, which were shot when following the same dam. When these brown bears have coarser hair than usual their skins are with difficulty to be distinguished from those of certain varieties of the grisly. Moreover, all bears vary greatly in size; and I have seen the bodies of very large black or brown bears with short fore-claws which were fully as heavy as, or perhaps heavier than, some small but full-grown grislies with long fore-claws. These very large bears with short claws are very reluctant to climb a tree; and are almost as clumsy about it as is a young grisly. Among the grislies the fur varies much in color and texture even among bears of the same locality; it is of course richest in the deep forest, while the bears of the dry plains and mountains are of a lighter, more washed-out hue.

A full grown grisly will usually weigh from five to seven hundred pounds; but exceptional individuals undoubtedly reach more than twelve hundredweight. The California bears are said to be much the largest. This I think is so, but I cannot say it with certainty—at any rate I have examined several skins of full-grown California bears which were no larger than those of many I have seen from the northern Rockies. The Alaskan bears, particularly those of the peninsula, are even bigger beasts; the skin of one which I saw in the possession of Mr. Webster, the taxidermist, was a good deal larger than the average polar bear skin; and the animal when alive, if in good condition, could hardly have weighed less than 1,400 pounds.[1] Bears vary wonderfully in weight, even to the extent of becoming half as heavy again, according as they are fat or lean; in this respect they are more like hogs than like any other animals.

The grisly is now chiefly a beast of the high hills and heavy timber; but this is merely because he has learned that he must rely on cover to guard him from man, and has forsaken the open ground accordingly. In old days, and in one or two very out-of-the-way places almost to the present time, he wandered at will over the plains. It is only the wariness born of fear which nowadays causes him to cling to the thick brush of the large river-bottoms through-out the plains country. When there were no rifle-bearing hunters in the land, to harass him and make him afraid, he roved hither and thither at will, in burly self-confidence. Then he cared little for cover, unless as a weather-break, or because it happened to contain food he liked. If the humor seized him he would roam for days over the rolling or broken prairie, searching for roots, digging up gophers, or perhaps following the great buffalo herds either to prey on some unwary straggler which he was able to catch at a disadvantage in a washout, or else to feast on the carcasses of those which died by accident. Old hunters, survivors of the long-vanished ages when the vast herds thronged the high plains and were followed by the wild red tribes, and by bands of whites who were scarcely less savage, have told me that they often met bears under such circumstances; and these bears were accustomed to sleep in a patch of rank sage brush, in the niche of a washout, or under the lee of a boulder, seeking their food abroad even in full daylight. The bears of the Upper Missouri basin — which were so light in color that the early explorers often alluded to them as gray or even as "white" — were particularly given to this life in the open. To this day that close kinsman of the grisly known as the bear of the barren grounds continues to lead this same kind of life, in the far north. My friend Mr. Rockhill, of Maryland, who was the first white man to explore eastern Tibet, describes the large, grisly-like bear of those desolate uplands as having similar habits.

However, the grisly is a shrewd beast and shows the usual bear-like capacity for adapting himself to changed conditions. He has in most places become a cover-haunting animal, sly in his ways, wary to a degree, and clinging to the shelter of the deepest forests in the mountains and of the most tangled thickets in the plains. Hence he has held his own far better than such game as the bison and elk. He is much less common than formerly, but he is still to be found throughout most of his former range; save of course in the immediate neighborhood of the large towns.

In most places the grisly hibernates, or as old hunters say "holes up," during the cold season, precisely as does the black bear; but as with the latter species, those animals which live furthest south spend the whole year abroad in mild seasons. The grisly rarely chooses that favorite den of his little black brother, a hollow tree or log, for his winter sleep, seeking or making some cavernous hole in the ground instead. The hole is sometimes in a slight hillock in a river bottom, but more often on a hillside, and may be either shallow or deep. In the mountains it is generally a natural cave in the rock, but among the foothills and on the plains the bear usually has to take some hollow or opening, and then fashion it into a burrow to his liking with his big digging claws.

Before the cold weather sets in the bear begins to grow restless, and to roam about seeking for a good place in which to hole up. One will often try and abandon several caves or partially dug-out burrows in succession before finding a place to its taste. It always endeavors to choose a spot where there is little chance of discovery or molestation, taking great care to avoid leaving too evident trace of its work. Hence it is not often that the dens are found.

Once in its den the bear passes the cold months in lethargic sleep; yet, in all but the coldest weather, and sometimes even then, its slumber is but light, and if disturbed it will promptly leave its den, prepared for fight or flight as the occasion may require. Many times when a hunter has stumbled on the winter resting-place of a bear and has left it, as he thought, without his presence being discovered, he has returned only to find that the crafty old fellow was aware of the danger all the time, and sneaked off as soon as the coast was clear. But in very cold weather hibernating bears can hardly be wakened from their torpid lethargy.

The length of time a bear stays in its den depends of course upon the severity of the season and the latitude and altitude of the country. In the northernmost and coldest regions all the bears hole up, and spend half the year in a state of lethargy; whereas in the South only the shes with young and the fat he-bears retire for the sleep, and these but for a few weeks, and only if the season is severe.

When the bear first leaves its den the fur is in very fine order, but it speedily becomes thin and poor, and does not recover its condition until the fall. Sometimes the bear does not betray any great hunger for a few days after its appearance; but in a short while it becomes ravenous. During the early spring, when the woods are still entirely barren and lifeless, while the snow yet lies in deep drifts, the lean, hungry brute, both maddened and weakened by long fasting, is more of a flesh eater than at any other time. It is at this period that it is most apt to turn true beast of prey, and show its prowess either at the expense of the wild game, or of the flocks of the settler and the herds of the ranchman. Bears are very capricious in this respect, however. Some are confirmed game and cattle killers; others are not; while yet others either are or are not accordingly as the freak seizes them, and their ravages vary almost unaccountably, both with the season and the locality.

Throughout 1889, for instance, no cattle, so far as I heard, were killed by bears anywhere near my range on the Little Missouri in western Dakota; yet I happened to know that during that same season the ravages of the bears among the herds of the cowmen in the Big Hole Basin, in western Montana, were very destructive.

In the spring and early summer of 1888, the bears killed no cattle near my ranch; but in the late summer and early fall of that year a big bear, which we well knew by its tracks, suddenly took to cattle-killing. This was a brute which had its headquarters on some very large brush bottoms a dozen miles below my ranch house, and which ranged to and fro across the broken country flanking the river on each side. It began just before berry time, but continued its career of destruction long after the wild plums and even buffalo berries had ripened. I think that what started it was a feast on a cow which had mired and died in the bed of the creek; at least it was not until after we found that it had been feeding at the carcass and had eaten every scrap, that we discovered traces of its ravages among the livestock. It seemed to attack the animals wholly regardless of their size and strength; its victims including a large bull and a beef steer, as well as cows, yearlings, and gaunt, weak trail "dough-gies," which had been brought in very late by a Texas cow-outfit—for that year several herds were driven up from the overstocked, eaten-out, and drought-stricken ranges of the far South. Judging from the signs, the crafty old grisly, as cunning as he was ferocious, usually lay in wait for the cattle when they came down to water, choosing some thicket of dense underbrush and twisted cottonwoods through which they had to pass before reaching the sand banks on the river's brink. Sometimes he pounced on them as they fed through the thick, low cover of the bottoms, where an assailant could either lie in ambush by one of the numerous cattle trails, or else creep unobserved toward some browsing beast. When within a few feet a quick rush carried him fairly on the terrified quarry; and though but a clumsy animal compared to the great cats, the grisly is far quicker than one would imagine from viewing his ordinary lumbering gait. In one or two instances the bear had apparently grappled with his victim by seizing it near the loins and striking a disabling blow over the small of the back; in at least one instance he had jumped on the animal's head, grasping it with his fore-paws, while with his fangs he tore open the throat or crunched the neck bone. Some of his victims were slain far from the river, in winding, brushy coulies of the Bad Lands, where the broken nature of the ground rendered stalking easy. Several of the ranchmen, angered at their losses, hunted their foe eagerly, but always with ill success; until one of them put poison in a carcass, and thus at last, in ignoble fashion, slew the cattle-killer.

Mr. Clarence King informs me that he was once eye-witness to a bear's killing a steer, in California. The steer was in a small pasture, and the bear climbed over, partly breaking down the rails which barred the gateway. The steer started to run, but the grisly overtook it in four or five bounds, and struck it a tremendous blow on the flank with one paw, knocking several ribs clear away from the spine, and killing the animal outright by the shock.

Horses no less than horned cattle at times fall victims to this great bear, which usually springs on them from the edge of a clearing as they graze in some mountain pasture, or among the foothills; and there is no other animal of which horses seem so much afraid. Generally the bear, whether successful or unsuccessful in its raids on cattle and horses, comes off unscathed from the struggle; but this is not always the case, and it has much respect for the hoofs or horns of its should-be prey. Some horses do not seem to know how to fight it at all; but others are both quick and vicious, and prove themselves very formidable foes, lashing out behind, and striking with their fore-hoofs. I have elsewhere given an instance of a stallion which beat off a bear, breaking its jaw.

Quite near my ranch, once, a cowboy in my employ found unmistakable evidence of the discomfiture of a bear by a long-horned range cow. It was in the early spring, and the cow with her new-born calf was in a brush-bordered valley. The footprints in the damp soil were very plain, and showed all that had happened. The bear had evidently come out of the bushes with a rush, probably bent merely on seizing the calf; and had slowed up when the cow instead of flying faced him. He had then begun to walk round his expected dinner in a circle, the cow fronting him and moving nervously back and forth, so that her sharp hoofs cut and trampled the ground. Finally she had charged savagely; whereupon the bear had bolted; and, whether frightened at the charge, or at the approach of some one, he had not returned.

The grisly is even fonder of sheep and pigs than is its smaller black brother. Lurking round the settler's house until after nightfall, it will vault into the fold or sty, grasp a helpless, bleating fleece-bearer, or a shrieking, struggling member of the bristly brotherhood, and bundle it out over the fence to its death. In carrying its prey a bear sometimes holds the body in its teeth, walking along on all-fours and dragging it as a wolf does. Sometimes, however, it seizes an animal in its forearms or in one of them, and walks awkwardly on three legs or two, adopting this method in lifting and pushing the body over rocks and down timber.

When a grisly can get at domestic animals it rarely seeks to molest game, the former being far less wary and more helpless. Its heaviness and clumsiness do not fit it well for a life of rapine against shy woodland creatures. Its vast strength and determined temper, however, more than make amends for lack of agility in the actual struggle with the stricken prey; its difficulty lies in seizing, not in killing, the game. Hence, when a grisly does take to game-killing, it is likely to attack bison, moose, and elk; it is rarely able to catch deer, still less sheep or antelope. In fact these smaller game animals often show but little dread of its neighborhood, and, though careful not to let it come too near, go on grazing when a bear is in full sight. Whitetail deer are frequently found at home in the same thicket in which a bear has its den, while they immediately desert the temporary abiding place of a wolf or cougar. Nevertheless, they sometimes presume too much on this confidence. A couple of years before the occurrence of the feats of cattle-killing mentioned above as happening near my ranch, either the same bear that figured in them, or another of similar tastes, took to game-hunting. The beast lived in the same succession of huge thickets which cover for two or three miles the river bottoms and the mouths of the inflowing creeks; and he suddenly made a raid on the whitetail deer which were plentiful in the dense cover. The shaggy, clumsy monster was cunning enough to kill several of these knowing creatures. The exact course of procedure I never could find out; but apparently the bear lay in wait beside the game trails, along which the deer wandered.

In the old days when the innumerable bison grazed free on the prairie, the grisly sometimes harassed their bands as it now does the herds of the ranchman. The bison was the most easily approached of all game, and the great bear could often get near some outlying straggler, in its quest after stray cows, yearlings, or calves. In default of a favorable chance to make a prey of one of these weaker members of the herds, it did not hesitate to attack the mighty bulls themselves; and perhaps the grandest sight which it was ever the good fortune of the early hunters to witness was one of these rare battles between a hungry grisly and a powerful buffalo bull. Nowadays, however, the few last survivors of the bison are vanishing even from the inaccessible mountain fastnesses in which they sought a final refuge from their destroyers.

At present the wapiti is of all wild game that which is most likely to fall a victim to the grisly, when the big bear is in the mood to turn hunter. Wapiti are found in the same places as the grisly, and in some spots they are yet very plentiful; they are less shy and active than deer, while not powerful enough to beat off so ponderous a foe; and they live in cover where there is always a good chance either to stalk or to stumble on them. At almost any season bear will come and feast on an elk carcass; and if the food supply runs short, in early spring, or in a fall when the berry crop falls, they sometimes have to do their own killing. Twice I have come across the remains of elk, which had seemingly been slain and devoured by bears. I have never heard of elk making a fight against a bear; yet, at close quarters and at bay, a bull elk in the rutting season is an ugly foe.

A bull moose is even more formidable, being able to strike the most lightning-like blows with his terrible forefeet, his true weapons of defense. I doubt if any beast of prey would rush in on one of these woodland giants, when his horns were grown, and if he was on his guard and bent on fight. Nevertheless, the moose sometimes fall victims to the uncouth prowess of the grisly, in the thick wet forests of the high northern Rockies, where both beasts dwell. An old hunter who a dozen years ago wintered at Jackson Lake, in northwestern Wyoming, told me that when the snows got deep on the mountains the moose came down and took up their abode near the lake, on its western side. Nothing molested them during the winter. Early in the spring a grisly came out of its den, and he found its tracks in many places, as it roamed restlessly about, evidently very hungry. Finding little to eat in the bleak, snow-drifted woods, it soon began to deprecate the moose, and killed two or three, generally by lying in wait and dashing out on them as they passed near its lurking-place. Even the bulls were at that season weak, and of course hornless, with small desire to fight; and in each case the rush of the great bear—doubtless made with the ferocity and speed which so often belie the seeming awkwardness of the animal—bore down the startled victim, taken utterly unawares before it had a chance to defend itself. In one case the bear had missed its spring; the moose going off, for a few rods, with huge jumps, and then settling down into its characteristic trot. The old hunter who followed the tracks said he would never have deemed it possible for any animal to make such strides while in a trot.

Nevertheless, the grisly is only occasionally, not normally, a formidable predatory beast, a killer of cattle and of large game. Although capable of far swifter movement than is promised by his frame of seemingly clumsy strength, and in spite of his power of charging with astonishing suddenness and speed, he yet lacks altogether the supple agility of such finished destroyers as the cougar and the wolf; and for the absence of this quality no amount of mere huge muscle can atone. He is more apt to feast on animals which have met their death by accident, or which have been killed by other beasts or by man, than to do his own killing. He is a very foul feeder, with a strong relish for carrion, and possesses a gruesome and cannibal fondness for the flesh of his own kind; a bear carcass will toll a brother bear to the ambushed hunter better than almost any other bait, unless it is the carcass of a horse.

Nor do these big bears always content themselves merely with the carcasses of their brethren. A black bear would have a poor chance if in the clutches of a large, hungry grisly; and an old male will kill and eat a cub, especially if he finds it at a disadvantage. A rather remarkable instance of this occurred in Yellowstone National Park, in the spring of 1891. The incident is related in the following letter written to Mr. William Hallett Phillips, of Washington, by another friend, Mr. Elwood Hofer. Hofer is an old mountain-man; I have hunted with him myself, and know his statements to be trustworthy. He was, at the time, at work in the Park getting animals for the National Museum at Washington, and was staying at Yancey's "hotel" near Tower Falls. His letter, which was dated June 21st, 1891, runs in part as follows:

"I had a splendid Grizzly or Roachback cub and was going to send him into the Springs next morning the team was here, I heard a racket outside went out and found him dead an old bear that made a 9 1-2 inch track had killed and partly eaten him. Last night another one came, one that made an 8 1-2 inch track, and broke Yancy up in the milk business. You know how the cabins stand here. There is a hitching-post between the saloon and old house, the little bear was killed there. In a creek close by was a milk house, last night another bear came there and smashed the whole thing up, leaving nothing but a few flattened buckets and pans and boards. I was sleeping in the old cabin, I heard the tin ware rattle but thought it was all right, supposed it was cows or horses about. I don't care about the milk but the damn cuss dug up the remains of the cub I had buried in the old ditch, he visited the old meat house but found nothing. Bear are very thick in this part of the Park, and are getting very fresh. I sent in the game to Capt. Anderson, hear it's doing well."

Grislies are fond of fish; and on the Pacific slope, where the salmon run, they, like so many other beasts, travel many scores of miles and crowd down to the rivers to gorge themselves upon the fish which are thrown up on the banks. Wading into the water a bear will knock out the salmon right and left when they are running thick.

Flesh and fish do not constitute the grisly's ordinary diet. At most times the big bear is a grubber in the ground, an eater of insects, roots, nuts, and berries. Its dangerous fore-claws are normally used to overturn stones and knock rotten logs to pieces, that it may lap up the small tribes of darkness which swarm under the one and in the other. It digs up the camas roots, wild onions, and an occasional luckless woodchuck or gopher. If food is very plenty bears are lazy, but commonly they are obliged to be very industrious, it being no light task to gather enough ants, beetles, crickets, tumble-bugs, roots, and nuts to satisfy the cravings of so huge a bulk. The sign of a bear's work is, of course, evident to the most unpracticed eye; and in no way can one get a better idea of the brute's power than by watching it busily working for its breakfast, shattering big logs and upsetting boulders by sheer strength. There is always a touch of the comic, as well as a touch of the strong and terrible, in a bear's look and actions. It will tug and pull, now with one paw, now with two, now on all fours, now on its hind legs, in the effort to turn over a large log or stone; and when it succeeds it jumps round to thrust its muzzle into the damp hollow and lap up the affrighted mice or beetles while they are still paralyzed by the sudden exposure.

The true time of plenty for bears is the berry season. Then they feast ravenously on huckleberries, blueberries, kinnikinnic berries, buffalo berries, wild plums, elderberries, and scores of other fruits. They often smash all the bushes in a berry patch, gathering the fruit with half-luxurious, half-laborious greed, sitting on their haunches, and sweeping the berries into their mouths with dexterous paws. So absorbed do they become in their feasts on the luscious fruit that they grow reckless of their safety, and feed in broad daylight, almost at midday; while in some of the thickets, especially those of the mountain haws, they make so much noise in smashing the branches that it is a comparatively easy matter to approach them unheard. That still-hunter is in luck who in the fall finds an accessible berry-covered hillside which is haunted by bears; but, as a rule, the berry bushes do not grow close enough together to give the hunter much chance.

Like most other wild animals, bears which have known the neighborhood of man are beasts of the darkness, or at least of the dusk and the gloaming. But they are by no means such true night-lovers as the big cats and the wolves. In regions where they know little of hunters they roam about freely in the daylight, and in cool weather are even apt to take their noontide slumbers basking in the sun. Where they are much hunted they finally almost reverse their natural habits and sleep throughout the hours of light, only venturing abroad after nightfall and before sunrise; but even yet this is not the habit of those bears which exist in the wilder localities where they are still plentiful. In these places they sleep, or at least rest, during the hours of greatest heat, and again in the middle part of the night, unless there is a full moon. They start on their rambles for food about mid-afternoon, and end their morning roaming soon after the sun is above the horizon. If the moon is full, however, they may feed all night long, and then wander but little in the daytime.

Aside from man, the full-grown grisly has hardly any foe to fear. Nevertheless, in the early spring, when weakened by the hunger that succeeds the winter sleep, it behooves even the grisly, if he dwells in the mountain fastnesses of the far Northwest, to beware of a famished troop of great timber wolves. These northern Rocky Mountain wolves are most formidable beasts, and when many of them band together in time of famine they do not hesitate to pounce on the black bear and cougar; and even a full-grown grisly is not safe from their attacks, unless he can back up against some rock which will prevent them from assailing him from behind. A small ranchman whom I knew well, who lived near Flathead Lake, once in April found where a troop of these wolves had killed a good-sized yearling grisly. Either cougar or wolf will make a prey of a grisly which is but a few months old; while any fox, lynx, wolverine, or fisher will seize the very young cubs. The old story about wolves fearing to feast on game killed by a grisly is all nonsense. Wolves are canny beasts, and they will not approach a carcass if they think a bear is hidden near by and likely to rush out at them; but under ordinary circumstances they will feast not only on the carcasses of the grisly's victims, but on the carcass of the grisly himself after he has been slain and left by the hunter. Of course wolves would only attack a grisly if in the most desperate straits for food, as even a victory over such an antagonist must be purchased with heavy loss of life; and a hungry grisly would devour either a wolf or a cougar, or any one of the smaller carnivora offhand, if it happened to corner it where it could not get away.

The grisly occasionally makes its den in a cave and spends therein the midday hours. But this is rare. Usually it lies in the dense shelter of the most tangled piece of woods in the neighborhood, choosing by preference some bit where the young growth is thick and the ground strewn with bowlders and fallen logs. Often, especially if in a restless mood and roaming much over the country, it merely makes a temporary bed, in which it lies but once or twice; and again it may make a more permanent lair or series of lairs, spending many consecutive nights in each. Usually the lair or bed is made some distance from the feeding ground; but bold bears, in very wild localities, may lie close by a carcass, or in the middle of a berry ground. The deer-killing bear above mentioned had evidently dragged two or three of his victims to his den, which was under an impenetrable mat of bullberries and dwarf box-alders, hemmed in by a cut bank on one side and a wall of gnarled cotton-woods on the other. Round this den, and rendering it noisome, were scattered the bones of several deer and a young steer or heifer. When we found it we thought we could easily kill the bear, but the fierce, cunning beast must have seen or smelt us, for though we lay in wait for it long and patiently, it did not come back to its place; nor, on our subsequent visits, did we ever find traces of its having done so.

Bear are fond of wallowing in the water, whether in the sand, on the edge of a rapid plains river, on the muddy margin of a pond, or in the oozy moss of a clear, cold mountain spring. One hot August afternoon, as I was clambering down a steep mountain-side near Pend'Oreille Lake, I heard a crash some distance below, which showed that a large beast was afoot. On making my way toward the spot, I found I had disturbed a big bear as it was lolling at ease in its bath; the discolored water showed where it had scrambled hastily out and galloped off as I approached. The spring welled out at the base of a high granite rock, forming a small pool of shimmering broken crystal. The soaked moss lay in a deep wet cushion round about, and jutted over the edges of the pool like a floating shelf. Graceful, water-loving ferns swayed to and fro. Above, the great conifers spread their murmuring branches, dimming the light, and keeping out the heat; their brown boles sprang from the ground like buttressed columns. On the barren mountain-side beyond the heat was oppressive. It was small wonder that Bruin should have sought the spot to cool his gross carcass in the fresh spring water.

The bear is a solitary beast, and although many may assemble together, in what looks like a drove, on some favorite feeding-ground—usually where the berries are thick, or by the banks of a salmon-thronged river—the association is never more than momentary, each going its own way as soon as its hunger is satisfied. The males always live alone by choice, save in the rutting season, when they seek the females. Then two or three may come together in the course of their pursuit and rough courtship of the female; and if the rivals are well matched, savage battles follow, so that many of the old males have their heads seamed with scars made by their fellows' teeth. At such times they are evil tempered and prone to attack man or beast upon the slightest provocation.

The she brings forth her cubs, one, two, or three in number, in her winter den. They are very small and helpless things, and it is some time after she leaves her winter home before they can follow her for any distance. They stay with her throughout the summer and the fall, leaving her when the cold weather sets in. By this time they are well grown; and hence, especially if an old male has joined the she, the family may number three or four individuals, so as to make what seems like quite a little troop of bears. A small ranchman who lived a dozen miles from me on the Little Missouri once found a she-bear and three half-grown cubs feeding at a berry-patch in a ravine. He shot the old she in the small of the back, whereat she made a loud roaring and squealing. One of the cubs rushed toward her; but its sympathy proved misplaced, for she knocked it over with a hearty cuff, either out of mere temper, or because she thought her pain must be due to an unprovoked assault from one of her offspring. The hunter then killed one of the cubs, and the other two escaped. When bears are together and one is wounded by a bullet, but does not see the real assailant, it often falls tooth and nail upon its comrade, apparently attributing its injury to the latter.

Bears are hunted in many ways. Some are killed by poison; but this plan is only practiced by the owners of cattle or sheep who have suffered from their ravages. Moreover, they are harder to poison than wolves. Most often they are killed in traps, which are sometimes dead-falls, on the principle of the little figure 4 trap familiar to every American country boy, sometimes log-pens in which the animal is taken alive, but generally huge steel gins. In some states there is a bounty for the destruction of grislies; and in many places their skins have a market price, although much less valuable than those of the black bear. The men who pursue them for the bounty, or for their fur, as well as the ranchmen who regard them as foes to stock, ordinarily use steel traps. The trap is very massive, needing no small strength to set, and it is usually chained to a bar or log of wood, which does not stop the bear's progress outright, but hampers and interferes with it, continually catching in tree stumps and the like. The animal when trapped makes off at once, biting at the trap and the bar; but it leaves a broad wake and sooner or later is found tangled up by the chain and bar. A bear is by no means so difficult to trap as a wolf or fox although more so than a cougar or a lynx. In wild regions a skilful trapper can often catch a great many with comparative ease. A cunning old grisly, however, soon learns the danger, and is then almost impossible to trap, as it either avoids the neighborhood altogether or finds out some way by which to get at the bait without springing the trap, or else deliberately springs it first. I have been told of bears which spring traps by rolling across them, the iron jaws slipping harmlessly off the big round body. An old horse is the most common bait.

It is, of course, all right to trap bears when they are followed merely as vermin or for the sake of the fur. Occasionally, however, hunters who are out merely for sport adopt this method; but this should never be done. To shoot a trapped bear for sport is a thoroughly unsportsmanlike proceeding. A funny plea sometimes advanced in its favor is that it is "dangerous." No doubt in exceptional instances this is true; exactly as it is true that in exceptional instances it is "dangerous" for a butcher to knock over a steer in the slaughterhouse. A bear caught only by the toes may wrench itself free as the hunter comes near, and attack him with pain-maddened fury; or if followed at once, and if the trap and bar are light, it may be found in some thicket, still free, and in a frenzy of rage. But even in such cases the beast has been crippled, and though crazy with pain and anger is easily dealt with by a good shot; while ordinarily the poor brute is found in the last stages of exhaustion, tied tight to a tree where the log or bar has caught, its teeth broken to splintered stumps by rabid snaps at the cruel trap and chain. Some trappers kill the trapped grislies with a revolver; so that it may easily be seen that the sport is not normally dangerous. Two of my own cowboys, Seawell and Dow, were originally from Maine, where they had trapped a number of black bears; and they always killed them either with a hatchet or a small 32-calibre revolver. One of them, Seawell, once came near being mauled by a trapped bear, seemingly at the last gasp, which he had approached most incautiously with his hatchet.

There is, however, one very real danger to which the solitary bear-trapper is exposed, the danger of being caught in his own trap. The huge jaws of the gin are easy to spring and most hard to open. If an unwary passer-by should tread between them and be caught by the leg, his fate would be doubtful, though he would probably die under the steadily growing torment of the merciless iron jaws, as they pressed ever deeper into the sore flesh and broken bones. But if caught by the arms, while setting or fixing the trap, his fate would be in no doubt at all, for it would be impossible for the stoutest man to free himself by any means. Terrible stories are told of solitary mountain hunters who disappeared, and were found years later in the lonely wilderness, as mouldering skeletons, the shattered bones of the forearms still held in the rusty jaws of the gin.

Doubtless the grisly could be successfully hunted with dogs, if the latter were carefully bred and trained to the purpose, but as yet this has not been done, and though dogs are sometimes used as adjuncts in grisly hunting they are rarely of much service. It is sometimes said that very small dogs are the best for this end. But this is only so with grislies that have never been hunted. In such a case the big bear sometimes becomes so irritated with the bouncing, yapping little terriers or fice-dogs that he may try to catch them and thus permit the hunter to creep up on him. But the minute he realizes, as he speedily does, that the man is his real foe, he pays no further heed whatever to the little dogs, who can then neither bring him to bay nor hinder his flight. Ordinary hounds, of the kinds used in the South for fox, deer, wildcat, and black bear, are but little better. I have known one or two men who at different times tried to hunt the grisly with a pack of hounds and fice-dogs wonted to the chase of the black bear, but they never met with success. This was probably largely owing to the nature of the country in which they hunted, a vast tangled mass of forest and craggy mountain; but it was also due to the utter inability of the dogs to stop the quarry from breaking bay when it wished. Several times a grisly was bayed, but always in some inaccessible spot which it took hard climbing to reach, and the dogs were never able to hold the beast until the hunters came up.

Still a well-trained pack of large hounds which were both bold and cunning could doubtless bay even a grisly. Such dogs are the big half-breed hounds sometimes used in the Alleghanies of West Virginia, which are trained not merely to nip a bear, but to grip him by the hock as he runs and either throw him or twirl him round. A grisly could not disregard a wary and powerful hound capable of performing this trick, even though he paid small heed to mere barking and occasional nipping. Nor do I doubt that it would be possible to get together a pack of many large fierce dogs, trained to dash straight at the head and hold on like a vise, which could fairly master a grisly and, though unable, of course, to kill him, would worry him breathless and hold him down so that he could be slain with ease. There have been instances in which five or six of the big so-called bloodhounds of the Southern States—not pure bloodhounds at all, but huge, fierce, ban-dogs, with a cross of the ferocious Cuban bloodhound, to give them good scenting powers—have by themselves mastered the cougar and the black bear. Such instances occurred in the hunting history of my own forefathers on my mother's side, who during the last half of the eighteenth, and the first half of the present, century lived in Georgia and over the border in what are now Alabama and Florida. These big dogs can only overcome such foes by rushing in in a body and grappling all together; if they hang back, lunging and snapping, a cougar or bear will destroy them one by one. With a quarry so huge and redoubtable as the grisly, no number of dogs, however large and fierce, could overcome him unless they all rushed on him in a mass, the first in the charge seizing by the head or throat. If the dogs hung back, or if there were only a few of them, or if they did not seize around the head, they would be destroyed without an effort. It is murder to slip merely one or two close-quarter dogs at a grisly. Twice I have known a man take a large bulldog with his pack when after one of these big bears and in each case the result was the same. In one instance the bear was trotting when the bulldog seized it by the cheek, and without so much as altering its gait, it brushed off the hanging dog with a blow from the forepaw that broke the latter's back. In the other instance the bear had come to bay, and when seized by the ear it got the dog's body up to its jaws, and tore out the life with one crunch.

A small number of dogs must rely on their activity, and must hamper the bear's escape by inflicting a severe bite and avoiding the counter-stroke. The only dog I ever heard of which, single-handed, was really of service in stopping a grisly, was a big Mexican sheepdog, once owned by the hunter Tazewell Woody. It was an agile beast with powerful jaws, and possessed both intelligence and a fierce, resolute temper. Woody killed three grislies with its aid. It attacked with equal caution and ferocity, rushing at the bear as the latter ran, and seizing the outstretched hock with a grip of iron, stopping the bear short, but letting go before the angry beast could whirl round and seize it. It was so active and wary that it always escaped damage; and it was so strong and bit so severely that the bear could not possibly run from it at any speed. In consequence, if it once came to close quarters with its quarry, Woody could always get near enough for a shot.

Hitherto, however, the mountain hunters—as distinguished from the trappers—who have followed the grisly have relied almost solely on their rifles. In my own case about half the bears I have killed I stumbled across almost by accident; and probably this proportion holds good generally. The hunter may be after bear at the time, or he may be after black-tail deer or elk, the common game in most of the haunts of the grisly; or he may merely be traveling through the country or prospecting for gold. Suddenly he comes over the edge of a cut bank, or round the sharp spur of a mountain or the shoulder of a cliff which walls in a ravine, or else the indistinct game trail he has been following through the great trees twists sharply to one side to avoid a rock or a mass of down timber, and behold he surprises old Ephraim digging for roots, or munching berries, or slouching along the path, or perhaps rising suddenly from the lush, rank plants amid which he has been lying. Or it may be that the bear will be spied afar rooting in an open glade or on a bare hill-side.

In the still-hunt proper it is necessary to find some favorite feeding ground, where there are many roots or berry-bearing bushes, or else to lure the grisly to a carcass. This last method of "baiting" for bear is under ordinary circumstances the only way which affords even a moderately fair chance of killing them. They are very cunning, with the sharpest of noses, and where they have had experience of hunters they dwell only in cover where it is almost impossible for the best still-hunters to approach them.

Nevertheless, in favorable ground a man can often find and kill them by fair stalking, in berry time, or more especially in the early spring, before the snow has gone from the mountains, and while the bears are driven by hunger to roam much abroad and sometimes to seek their food in the open. In such cases the still-hunter is stirring by the earliest dawn, and walks with stealthy speed to some high point of observation from which he can overlook the feeding-grounds where he has previously discovered sign. From this point of vantage he scans the country far and near, either with his own keen eyes or with powerful glasses; and he must combine patience and good sight with the ability to traverse long distances noiselessly and yet at speed. He may spend two or three hours sitting still and looking over a vast tract of country before he will suddenly spy a bear; or he may see nothing after the most careful search in a given place, and must then go on half a dozen miles to another, watching warily as he walks, and continuing this possibly for several days before getting a glimpse of his game. If the bear are digging roots, or otherwise procuring their food on the bare hill sides and table-lands, it is of course comparatively easy to see them; and it is under such circumstances that this kind of hunting is most successful. Once seen, the actual stalk may take two or three hours, the nature of the ground and the direction of the wind often necessitating a long circuit; perhaps a gully, a rock, or a fallen log offers a chance for an approach to within two hundred yards, and although the hunter will, if possible, get much closer than this, yet even at such a distance a bear is a large enough mark to warrant risking a shot.

Usually the berry grounds do not offer such favorable opportunities, as they often lie in thick timber, or are covered so densely with bushes as to obstruct the view; and they are rarely commanded by a favorable spot from which to spy. On the other hand, as already said, bears occasionally forget all their watchfulness while devouring fruit, and make such a noise rending and tearing the bushes that, if once found, a man can creep upon them unobserved.

CHAPTER IV

HUNTING THE GRISLY

IF out in the late fall or early spring, it is often possible to follow a bear's trail in the snow; having come upon it either by chance or hard hunting, or else having found where it leads from some carcass on which the beast has been feeding. In the pursuit one must exercise great caution, as at such times the hunter is easily seen a long way off, and game is always especially watchful for any foe that may follow its trail.

Once I killed a grisly in this manner. It was early in the fall, but snow lay on the ground, while the gray weather boded a storm. My camp was in a bleak, wind-swept valley, high among the mountains which form the divide between the headwaters of the Salmon and Clark's Fork of the Columbia. All night I had lain in my buffalo-bag, under the lee of a windbreak of branches, in the clump of fir-trees, where I had halted the preceding evening. At my feet ran a rapid mountain torrent, its bed choked with ice-covered rocks; I had been lulled to sleep by the stream's splashing murmur, and the loud moaning of the wind along the naked cliffs. At dawn I rose and shook myself free of the buffalo robe, coated with hoar-frost. The ashes of the fire were lifeless; in the dim morning the air was bitter cold. I did not linger a moment, but snatched up my rifle, pulled on my fur cap and gloves and strode off up a side ravine; as I walked I ate some mouthfuls of venison, left over from supper.

Two hours of toil up the steep mountain brought me to the top of a spur. The sun had risen, but was hidden behind a bank of sullen clouds. On the divide I halted, and gazed out over a vast landscape, inconceivably wild and dismal. Around me towered the stupendous mountain masses which make up the backbone of the Rockies. From my feet, as far as I could see, stretched a rugged and barren chaos of ridges and detached rock masses. Behind me, far below, the stream wound like a silver ribbon, fringed with dark conifers and the changing, dying foliage of poplar and quaking aspen. In front the bottoms of the valleys were filled with the sombre evergreen forest, dotted here and there with black, ice-skimmed tarns; and the dark spruces clustered also in the higher gorges, and were scattered thinly along the mountain sides. The snow which had fallen lay in drifts and streaks, while where the wind had scope it was blown off, and the ground left bare.

For two hours I walked onward across the ridges and valleys. Then among some scattered spruces, where the snow lay to the depth of half a foot, I suddenly came on the fresh, broad trail of a grisly. The brute was evidently roaming restlessly about in search of a winter den, but willing, in passing, to pick up any food that lay handy. At once I took the trail, traveling above and to one side, and keeping a sharp lookout ahead. The bear was going across wind, and this made my task easy. I walked rapidly, though cautiously; and it was only in crossing the large patches of bare ground that I had to fear making a noise. Elsewhere the snow muffled my footsteps, and made the trail so plain that I scarcely had to waste a glance upon it, bending my eyes always to the front.

At last, peering cautiously over a ridge crowned with broken rocks, I saw my quarry, a big, burly bear, with silvered fur. He had halted on an open hillside, and was busily digging up the caches of some rock gophers or squirrels. He seemed absorbed in his work, and the stalk was easy. Slipping quietly back, I ran toward the end of the spur, and in ten minutes struck a ravine, of which one branch ran past within seventy yards of where the bear was working. In this ravine was a rather close growth of stunted evergreens, affording good cover, although in one or two places I had to lie down and crawl through the snow. When I reached the point for which I was aiming, the bear had just finished rooting, and was starting off. A slight whistle brought him to a standstill, and I drew a bead behind his shoulder, and low down, resting the rifle across the crooked branch of a dwarf spruce. At the crack he ran off at speed, making no sound, but the thick spatter of blood splashes, showing clear on the white snow, betrayed the mortal nature of the wound. For some minutes I followed the trail; and then, topping a ridge, I saw the dark bulk lying motionless in a snowdrift at the foot of a low rock-wall, down which he had tumbled.

The usual practice of the still-hunter who is after grisly is to toll it to baits. The hunter either lies in ambush near the carcass, or approaches it stealthily when he thinks the bear is at its meal.

One day while camped near the Bitter Root Mountains in Montana I found that a bear had been feeding on the carcass of a moose which lay some five miles from the little open glade in which my tent was pitched, and I made up my mind to try to get a shot at it that afternoon. I stayed in camp till about three o'clock, lying lazily back on the bed of sweet-smelling evergreen boughs, watching the pack ponies as they stood under the pines on the edge of the open, stamping now and then, and switching their tails. The air was still, the sky a glorious blue; at that hour in the afternoon even the September sun was hot. The smoke from the smouldering logs of the camp fire curled thinly upward. Little chipmunks scuttled out from their holes to the packs, which lay in a heap on the ground, and then scuttled madly back again. A couple of drab-colored whiskey-jacks, with bold mien and fearless bright eyes, hopped and fluttered round, picking up the scraps, and uttering an extraordinary variety of notes, mostly discordant; so tame were they that one of them lit on my outstretched arm as I half dozed, basking in the sunshine.

When the shadows began to lengthen, I shouldered my rifle and plunged into the woods. At first my route lay along a mountain side; then for half a mile over a windfall, the dead timber piled about in crazy confusion. After that I went up the bottom of a valley by a little brook, the ground being carpeted with a sponge of soaked moss. At the head of this brook was a pond covered with water-lilies; and a scramble through a rocky pass took me into a high, wet valley, where the thick growth of spruce was broken by occasional strips of meadow. In this valley the moose carcass lay, well at the upper end.

In moccasined feet I trod softly through the soundless woods. Under the dark branches it was already dusk, and the air had the cool chill of evening. As I neared the clump where the body lay, I walked with redoubled caution, watching and listening with strained alertness. Then I heard a twig snap; and my blood leaped, for I knew the bear was at his supper. In another moment I saw his shaggy, brown form. He was working with all his awkward giant strength, trying to bury the carcass, twisting it to one side and the other with wonderful ease. Once he got angry and suddenly gave it a tremendous cuff with his paw; in his bearing he had something half humorous, half devilish. I crept up within forty yards; but for several minutes he would not keep his head still. Then something attracted his attention in the forest, and he stood motionless looking toward it, broadside to me, with his forepaws planted on the carcass. This gave me my chance. I drew a very fine bead between his eye and ear, and pulled the trigger. He dropped like a steer when struck with a pole-axe.

If there is a good hiding-place handy it is better to lie in wait at the carcass. One day on the headwaters of the Madison, I found that a bear was coming to an elk I had shot some days before; and I at once determined to ambush the beast when he came back that evening. The carcass lay in the middle of a valley a quarter of a mile broad. The bottom of this valley was covered by an open forest of tall pines; a thick jungle of smaller evergreens marked where the mountains rose on either hand. There were a number of large rocks scattered here and there, one, of very convenient shape, being only some seventy or eighty yards from the carcass. Up this I clambered. It hid me perfectly, and on its top was a carpet of soft pine needles, on which I could lie at my ease.

Hour after hour passed by. A little black woodpecker with a yellow crest ran nimbly up and down the tree-trunks for some time and then flitted away with a party of chickadees and nut-hatches. Occasionally a Clark's crow soared about overhead or clung in any position to the swaying end of a pine branch, chattering and screaming. Flocks of crossbills, with wavy flight and plaintive calls, flew to a small mineral lick near by, where they scraped the clay with their queer little beaks.

As the westering sun sank out of sight beyond the mountains these sounds of bird-life gradually died away. Under the great pines the evening was still with the silence of primeval desolation. The sense of sadness and loneliness, the melancholy of the wilderness, came over me like a spell. Every slight noise made my pulses throb as I lay motionless on the rock gazing intently into the gathering gloom. I began to fear that it would grow too dark to shoot before the grisly came.

Suddenly and without warning, the great bear stepped out of the bushes and trod across the pine needles with such swift and silent footsteps that its bulk seemed unreal. It was very cautious, continually halting to peer around; and once it stood up on its hind legs and looked long down the valley toward the red west. As it reached the carcass I put a bullet between its shoulders. It rolled over, while the woods resounded with its savage roaring. Immediately it struggled to its feet and staggered off; and fell again to the next shot, squalling and yelling. Twice this was repeated; the brute being one of those bears which greet every wound with a great outcry, and sometimes seem to lose their feet when hit—although they will occasionally fight as savagely as their more silent brethren. In this case, the wounds were mortal, and the bear died before reaching the edge of the thicket.

I spent much of the fall of 1889 hunting on the headwaters of the Salmon and Snake in Idaho, and along the Montana boundary line from the Big Hole Basin and the head of the Wisdom River to the neighborhood of Red Rock Pass and to the north and west of Henry's Lake. During the last fortnight my companion was the old mountain man, already mentioned, name Griffeth or Griffin—I cannot tell which, as he was always called either "Hank" or "Griff." He was a crabbedly honest old fellow, and a very skilful hunter; but he was worn out with age and rheumatism, and his temper had failed even faster than his bodily strength. He showed me a greater variety of game than I had ever seen before in so short a time; nor did I ever before or after make so successful a hunt. But he was an exceedingly disagreeable companion on account of his surly, moody ways. I generally had to get up first, to kindle the fire and make ready breakfast, and he was very quarrelsome. Finally, during my absence from camp one day, while not very far from Red Rock Pass, he found my whiskey-flask, which I kept purely for emergencies, and drank all the contents. When I came back he was quite drunk. This was unbearable, and after some high words I left him, and struck off homeward through the woods on my own account. We had with us four pack and saddle horses; and of these I took a very intelligent and gentle little bronco mare, which possessed the invaluable trait of always staying near camp, even when not hobbled. I was not hampered with much of an outfit, having only my buffalo sleeping-bag, a fur coat, and my washing kit, with a couple of spare pairs of socks and some handkerchiefs. A frying-pan, some salt, flour, baking-powder, a small chunk of salt pork, and a hatchet, made up a light pack, which, with the bedding, I fastened across the stock saddle by means of a rope and a spare packing cinch. My cartridges and knife were in my belt; my compass and matches, as always, in my pocket. I walked, while the little mare followed almost like a dog, often without my having to hold the lariat which served as halter.

The country was for the most part fairly open, as I kept near the foothills where glades and little prairies broke the pine forest. The trees were of small size. There was no regular trail, but the course was easy to keep, and I had no trouble of any kind save on the second day. That afternoon I was following a stream which at last "canyoned up," that is, sank to the bottom of a canyon-like ravine impassable for a horse. I started up a side valley, intending to cross from its head coulies to those of another valley which would lead in below the canyon.

However, I got enmeshed in the tangle of winding valleys at the foot of the steep mountains, and as dusk was coming on I halted and camped in a little open spot by the side of a small, noisy brook, with crystal water. The place was carpeted with soft, wet, green moss, dotted red with the kinnikinnic berries, and at its edge, under the trees where the ground was dry, I threw down the buffalo bed on the mat of sweet-smelling pine needles. Making camp took but a moment. I opened the pack, tossed the bedding on a smooth spot, knee-haltered the little mare, dragged up a few dry logs, and then strolled off, rifle on shoulder, through the frosty gloaming, to see if I could pick up a grouse for supper.

For half a mile I walked quickly and silently over the pine needles, across a succession of slight ridges separated by narrow, shallow valleys. The forest here was composed of lodge-pole pines, which on the ridges grew close together, with tall slender trunks, while in the valleys the growth was more open. Though the sun was behind the mountains there was yet plenty of light by which to shoot, but it was fading rapidly.

At last, as I was thinking of turning toward camp, I stole up to the crest of one of the ridges, and looked over into the valley some sixty yards off. Immediately I caught the loom of some large, dark object; and another glance showed me a big grisly walking slowly off with his head down. He was quartering to me, and I fired into his flank, the bullet, as I afterward found, ranging forward and piercing one lung. At the shot he uttered a loud, moaning grunt and plunged forward at a heavy gallop, while I raced obliquely down the hill to cut him off. After going a few hundred feet he reached a laurel thicket, some thirty yards broad, and two or three times as long, which he did not leave. I ran up to the edge and there halted, not liking to venture into the mass of twisted, close-growing stems and glossy foliage. Moreover, as I halted, I heard him utter a peculiar, savage kind of whine from the heart of the brush. Accordingly, I began to skirt the edge, standing on tiptoe and gazing earnestly to see if I could not catch a glimpse of his hide. When I was at the narrowest part of the thicket, he suddenly left it directly opposite, and then wheeled and stood broadside to me on the hillside, a little above. He turned his head stiffly toward me; scarlet strings of froth hung from his lips; his eyes burned like embers in the gloom.

I held true, aiming behind the shoulder, and my bullet shattered the point or lower end of his heart, taking out a big nick. Instantly the great bear turned with a harsh roar of fury and challenge, blowing the bloody foam from his mouth, so that I saw the gleam of his white fangs; and then he charged straight at me, crashing and bounding through the laurel bushes, so that it was hard to aim. I waited till he came to a fallen tree, raking him as he topped it with a ball, which entered his chest and went through the cavity of his body, but he neither swerved nor flinched, and at the moment I did not know that I had struck him. He came steadily on, and in another second was almost upon me. I fired for his forehead, but my bullet went low, entering his open mouth, smashing his lower jaw and going into the neck. I leaped to one side almost as I pulled the trigger; and through the hanging smoke the first thing I saw was his paw as he made a vicious side blow as me. The rush of his charge carried him past. As he struck he lurched forward, leaving a pool of bright blood where his muzzle hit the ground; but he recovered himself and made two or three jumps onward, while I hurriedly jammed a couple of cartridges into the magazine, my rifle holding only four, all of which I had fired. Then he tried to pull up, but as he did so his muscles seemed suddenly to give way, his head drooped, and he rolled over and over like a shot rabbit. Each of my first three bullets had inflicted a mortal wound.

It was already twilight, and I merely opened the carcass, and then trotted back to camp. Next morning I returned and with much labor took off the skin. The fur was very fine, the animal being in excellent trim, and unusually bright-colored. Unfortunately, in packing it out I lost the skull, and had to supply its place with one of plaster. The beauty of the trophy, and the memory of the circumstances under which I procured it, make me value it perhaps more highly than any other in my house.

This is the only instance in which I have been regularly charged by a grisly. On the whole, the danger of hunting these great bears has been much exaggerated. At the beginning of the present century, when white hunters first encountered the grisly, he was doubtless an exceedingly savage beast, prone to attack without provocation, and a redoubtable foe to persons armed with the clumsy, small bore, muzzle-loading rifles of the day. But at present bitter experience has taught him caution. He has been hunted for sport, and hunted for his pelt, and hunted for the bounty, and hunted as a dangerous enemy to stock, until, save in the very wildest districts, he has learned to be more wary than a deer, and to avoid man's presence almost as carefully as the most timid kind of game. Except in rare cases he will not attack of his own accord, and, as a rule, even when wounded, his object is escape rather than battle.

Still, when fairly brought to bay, or when moved by a sudden fit of ungovernable anger, the grisly is beyond peradventure a very dangerous antagonist. The first shot, if taken at a bear a good distance off and previously unwounded and unharried, is not usually fraught with much danger, the startled animal being at the outset bent merely on flight. It is always hazardous, however, to track a wounded and worried grisly into thick cover, and the man who habitually follows and kills this chief of American game in dense timber, never abandoning the bloody trail whithersoever it leads, must show no small degree of skill and hardihood, and must not too closely count the risk to life and limb. Bears differ widely in temper, and occasionally one may be found who will not show fight, no matter how much he is bullied; but, as a rule, a hunter must be cautious in meddling with a wounded animal which has retreated into a dense thicket, and has been once or twice roused; and such a beast, when it does turn, will usually charge again and again, and fight to the last with unconquerable ferocity. The short distance at which the bear can be seen through the underbrush, the fury of his charge, and his tenacity of life make it necessary for the hunter on such occasions to have steady nerves and a fairly quick and accurate aim. It is always well to have two men in following a wounded bear under such conditions. This is not necessary, however, and a good hunter, rather than lose his quarry, will, under ordinary circumstances, follow and attack it, no matter how tangled the fastness in which it has sought refuge; but he must act warily and with the utmost caution and resolution, if he wishes to escape a terrible and probably fatal mauling. An experienced hunter is rarely rash, and never heedless; he will not, when alone, follow a wounded bear into a thicket, if by the exercise of patience, skill, and knowledge of the game's habits he can avoid the necessity; but it is idle to talk of the feat as something which ought in no case to be attempted. While danger ought never to be needlessly incurred, it is yet true that the keenest zest in sport comes from its presence, and from the consequent exercise of the qualities necessary to overcome it. The most thrilling moments of an American hunter's life are those in which, with every sense on the alert, and with nerves strung to the highest point, he is following alone into the heart of its forest fastness the fresh and bloody footprints of an angered grisly; and no other triumph of American hunting can compare with the victory to be thus gained.

These big bears will not ordinarily charge from a distance of over a hundred yards; but there are exceptions to this rule. In the fall of 1890 my friend Archibald Rogers was hunting in Wyoming, south of the Yellowstone Park, and killed seven bears. One, an old he, was out on a bare tableland, grubbing for roots, when he was spied. It was early in the afternoon, and the hunters, who were on a high mountain slope, examined him for some time through their powerful glasses before making him out to be a bear. They then stalked up to the edge of the wood which fringed the tableland on one side, but could get no nearer than about three hundred yards, the plains being barren of all cover. After waiting for a couple of hours Rogers risked the shot, in despair of getting nearer, and wounded the bear, though not very seriously. The animal made off, almost broadside to, and Rogers ran forward to intercept it. As soon as it saw him, it turned and rushed straight for him, not heeding his second shot, and evidently bent on charging home. Rogers then waited until it was within twenty yards, and brained it with his third bullet.

In fact bears differ individually in courage and ferocity precisely as men do, or as the Spanish bulls, of which it is said that not more than one in twenty is fit to stand the combat of the arena. One grisly can scarcely be bullied into resistance; the next may fight to the end, against any odds, without flinching, or even attack unprovoked. Hence men of limited experience in this sport, generalizing from the actions of the two or three bears each has happened to see or kill, often reach diametrically opposite conclusions as to the fighting temper and capacity of the quarry. Even old hunters—who indeed, as a class, are very narrow-minded and opinionated—often generalize just as rashly as beginners. One will portray all bears as very dangerous; another will speak and act as if he deemed them of no more consequence than so many rabbits. I knew one old hunter who had killed a score without ever seeing one show fight. On the other hand, Dr. James C. Merrill, U. S. A., who has had about as much experience with bears as I have had, informs me that he has been charged with the utmost determination three times. In each case the attack was delivered before the bear was wounded or even shot at, the animal being roused by the approach of the hunters from his day bed, and charging headlong at them from a distance of twenty or thirty paces. All three bears were killed before they could do any damage. There was a very remarkable incident connected with the killing of one of them. It occurred in the northern spurs of the Bighorn range. Dr. Merrill, in company with an old hunter, had climbed down into a deep, narrow canyon. The bottom was threaded with well-beaten elk trails. While following one of these the two men turned a corner of the canyon and were instantly charged by an old she-grisly, so close that it was only by good luck that one of the hurried shots disabled her and caused her to tumble over a cut bank where she was easily finished. They found that she had been lying directly across the game trail, on a smooth well beaten patch of bare earth, which looked as if it had been dug up, refilled, and trampled down. Looking curiously at this patch they saw a bit of hide only partially covered at one end; digging down they found the body of a well grown grisly cub. Its skull had been crushed, and the brains licked out, and there were signs of other injuries. The hunters pondered long over this strange discovery, and hazarded many guesses as to its meaning. At last they decided that probably the cub had been killed, and its brains eaten out, either by some old male grisly or by a cougar, that the mother had returned and driven away the murderer, and that she had then buried the body and lain above it, waiting to wreak her vengeance on the first passer-by.

Old Tazewell Woody, during his thirty years' life as a hunter in the Rockies and on the great plains, killed very many grislies. He always exercised much caution in dealing with them; and, as it happened, he was by some suitable tree in almost every case when he was charged. He would accordingly climb the tree (a practice of which I do not approve however); and the bear would look up at him and pass on without stopping. Once, when he was hunting in the mountains with a companion, the latter, who was down in a valley, while Woody was on the hillside, shot at a bear. The first thing Woody knew the wounded grisly, running uphill, was almost on him from behind. As he turned it seized his rifle in its jaws. He wrenched the rifle round, while the bear still gripped it, and pulled trigger, sending a bullet into its shoulder; whereupon it struck him with its paw, and knocked him over the rocks. By good luck he fell in a snow bank and was not hurt in the least. Meanwhile the bear went on and they never got it.

Once he had an experience with a bear which showed a very curious mixture of rashness and cowardice. He and a companion were camped in a little tepee or wigwam, with a bright fire in front of it, lighting up the night. There was an inch of snow on the ground. Just after they went to bed a grisly came close to camp. Their dog rushed out and they could hear it bark round in the darkness for nearly an hour; then the bear drove it off and came right into camp. It went close to the fire, picking up the scraps of meat and bread, pulled a haunch of venison down from a tree, and passed and repassed in front of the tepee, paying no heed whatever to the two men, who crouched in the doorway talking to one another. Once it passed so close that Woody could almost touch it. Finally his companion fired into it, and off it ran, badly wounded, without an attempt at retaliation. Next morning they followed its tracks in the snow, and found it a quarter of a mile away. It was near a pine and had buried itself under the loose earth, pine needles, and snow; Woody's companion almost walked over it, and putting his rifle to its ear blew out its brains.

In all his experience Woody had personally seen but four men who were badly mauled by bears. Three of these were merely wounded. One was bitten terribly in the back. Another had an arm partially chewed off. The third was a man named George Dow, and the accident happened to him on the Yellowstone, about the year 1878. He was with a pack animal at the time, leading it on a trail through a wood. Seeing a big she-bear with cubs he yelled at her; whereat she ran away, but only to cache her cubs, and in a minute, having hidden them, came racing back at him. His pack animal being slow he started to climb a tree; but before he could get far enough up she caught him, almost biting a piece out of the calf of his leg, pulled him down, bit and cuffed him two or three times, and then went on her way.

The only time Woody ever saw a man killed by a bear was once when he had given a touch of variety to his life by shipping on a New Bedford whaler which had touched at one of the Puget Sound ports. The whaler went up to a part of Alaska where bears were very plentiful and bold. One day a couple of boats' crews landed; and the men, who were armed only with an occasional harpoon or lance, scattered over the beach, one of them, a Frenchman, wading into the water after shell-fish. Suddenly a bear emerged from some bushes and charged among the astonished sailors, who scattered in every direction; but the bear, said Woody, "just had it in for that Frenchman," and went straight at him. Shrieking with terror he retreated up to his neck in the water; but the bear plunged in after him, caught him, and disemboweled him. One of the Yankee mates then fired a bomb lance into the bear's hips, and the savage beast hobbled off into the dense cover of the low scrub, where the enraged sailor folk were unable to get at it.

The truth is that while the grisly generally avoids a battle if possible, and often acts with great cowardice, it is never safe to take liberties with him; he usually fights desperately and dies hard when wounded and cornered, and exceptional individuals take the aggressive on small provocation.

During the years I lived on the frontier I came in contact with many persons who had been severely mauled or even crippled for life by grislies; and a number of cases where they killed men outright were also brought under my ken. Generally these accidents, as was natural, occurred to hunters who had roused or wounded the game.

A fighting bear sometimes uses his claws and sometimes his teeth. I have never known one to attempt to kill an antagonist by hugging, in spite of the popular belief to this effect; though he will sometimes draw an enemy toward him with his paws the better to reach him with his teeth, and to hold him so that he cannot escape from the biting. Nor does the bear often advance on his hind legs to the attack; though, if the man has come close to him in thick underbrush, or has stumbled on him in his lair unawares, he will often rise up in this fashion and strike a single blow. He will also rise in clinching with a man on horseback. In 1882 a mounted Indian was killed in this manner on one of the river bottoms some miles below where my ranch house now stands, not far from the junction of the Beaver and Little Missouri. The bear had been hunted into a thicket by a band of Indians, in whose company my informant, a white squaw-man, with whom I afterward did some trading, was traveling. One of them in the excitement of the pursuit rode across the end of the thicket; as he did so the great beast sprang at him with wonderful quickness, rising on its hind legs, and knocking over the horse and rider with a single sweep of its terrible fore-paws. It then turned on the fallen man and tore him open, and though the other Indians came promptly to his rescue and slew his assailant, they were not in time to save their comrade's life.

A bear is apt to rely mainly on his teeth or claws according to whether his efforts are directed primarily to killing his foe or to making good his own escape. In the latter event he trusts chiefly to his claws. If cornered, he of course makes a rush for freedom, and in that case he downs any man who is in his way with a sweep of his great paw, but passes on without stopping to bite him. If while sleeping or resting in thick brush some one suddenly stumbles on him close up he pursues the same course, less from anger than from fear, being surprised and startled. Moreover, if attacked at close quarters by men and dogs he strikes right and left in defense.

Sometimes what is called a charge is rather an effort to get away. In localities where he has been hunted, a bear, like every other kind of game, is always on the lookout for an attack, and is prepared at any moment for immediate flight. He seems ever to have in his mind, whether feeding, sunning himself, or merely roaming around, the direction — usually toward the thickest cover or most broken ground — in which he intends to run if molested. When shot at he instantly starts toward this place; or he may be so confused that he simply runs he knows not whither; and in either event he may take a line that leads almost directly to or by the hunter, although he had at first no thought of charging. In such a case he usually strikes a single knock-down blow and gallops on without halting, though that one blow may have taken life. If the claws are long and fairly sharp (as in early spring, or even in the fall, if the animal has been working over soft ground) they add immensely to the effect of the blow, for they cut like blunt axes. Often, however, late in the season, and if the ground has been dry and hard, or rocky, the claws are worn down nearly to the quick, and the blow is then given mainly with the under side of the paw; although even under this disadvantage a thump from a big bear will down a horse or smash in a man's breast. The hunter Hofer once lost a horse in this manner. He shot at and wounded a bear which rushed off, as ill luck would have it, past the place where his horse was picketed; probably more in fright than in anger it struck the poor beast a blow which, in the end, proved mortal.

If a bear means mischief and charges not to escape but to do damage, its aim is to grapple with or throw down its foe and bite him to death. The charge is made at a gallop, the animal some-times coming on silently, with the mouth shut, and sometimes with the jaws open, the lips drawn back and teeth showing, utter-ing at the same time a succession of roars or of savage rasping snarls. Certain bears charge without any bluster and perfectly straight; while others first threaten and bully, and even when charging stop to growl, shake the head, and bite at a bush or knock holes in the ground with their fore-paws. Again, some of them charge home with a ferocious resolution which their extreme tenacity of life renders especially dangerous; while others can be turned or driven back even by a shot which is not mortal. They show the same variability in their behavior when wounded. Often a big bear, especially if charging, will receive a bullet in perfect silence, without flinching or seeming to pay any heed to it; while another will cry out and tumble about, and if charging, even though it may not abandon the attack, will pause for a moment to whine or bite at the wound.

Sometimes a single bite causes death. One of the most success-ful bear hunters I ever knew, an old fellow whose real name I never heard as he was always called Old Ike, was killed in this way in the spring or early summer of 1886 on one of the head-waters of the Salmon. He was a very good shot, had killed nearly a hun-dred bears with the rifle, and, although often charged, had never met with any accident, so that he had grown somewhat careless. On the day in question he had met a couple of mining prospec-tors and was traveling with them, when a grisly crossed his path.

The old hunter immediately ran after it, rapidly gaining, as the bear did not hurry when it saw itself pursued, but slouched slowly forward, occasionally turning its head to grin and growl. It soon went into a dense grove of young spruce, and as the hunter reached the edge it charged fiercely out. He fired one hasty shot, evidently wounding the animal, but not seriously enough to stop or cripple it; and as his two companions ran forward they saw the bear seize him with its widespread jaws, forcing him to the ground. They shouted and fired, and the beast abandoned the fallen man on the instant and sullenly retreated into the spruce thicket, whither they dared not follow it. Their friend was at his last gasp; for the whole side of the chest had been crushed in by the one bite, the lungs showing between the rent ribs.

Very often, however, a bear does not kill a man by one bite, but after throwing him lies on him, biting him to death. Usually, if no assistance is at hand, such a man is doomed; although if he pretends to be dead, and has the nerve to lie quiet under very rough treatment, it is just possible that the bear may leave him alive, perhaps after half burying what it believes to be the body. In a very few exceptional instances men of extraordinary prowess with the knife have succeeded in beating off a bear, and even in mortally wounding it, but in most cases a single-handed struggle, at close quarters, with a grisly bent on mischief, means death.

Occasionally the bear, although vicious, is also frightened, and passes on after giving one or two bites; and frequently a man who is knocked down is rescued by his friends before he is killed, the big beast mayhap using his weapons with clumsiness. So a bear may kill a foe with a single blow of its mighty forearm, either crushing in the head or chest by sheer force of sinew, or else tearing open the body with its formidable claws; and so on the other hand he may, and often does, merely disfigure or maim the foe by a hurried stroke. Hence it is common to see men who have escaped the clutches of a grisly, but only at the cost of features marred beyond recognition, or a body rendered almost helpless for life. Almost every old resident of western Montana or northern

Idaho has known two or three unfortunates who have suffered in this manner. I have myself met one such man in Helena, and another in Missoula; both were living at least as late as 1889, the date at which I last saw them. One had been partially scalped by a bear's teeth; the animal was very old and so the fangs did not enter the skull. The other had been bitten across the face, and the wounds never entirely healed, so that his disfigured visage was hideous to behold.

Most of these accidents occur in following a wounded or worried bear into thick cover; and under such circumstances an animal apparently hopelessly disabled, or in the death throes, may with a last effort kill one or more of its assailants. In 1874 my wife's uncle, Captain Alexander Moore, U. S. A., and my friend Captain Bates, with some men of the 2d and 3d Cavalry, were scouting in Wyoming, near the Freezeout Mountains. One morning they roused a bear in the open prairie and followed it at full speed as it ran toward a small creek. At one spot in the creek beavers had built a dam, and as usual in such places there was a thick growth of bushes and willow saplings. Just as the bear reached the edge of this little jungle it was struck by several balls, both of its forelegs being broken. Nevertheless, it managed to shove itself forward on its hind-legs, and partly rolled, partly pushed itself into the thicket, the bushes though low being so dense that its body was at once completely hidden. The thicket was a mere patch of brush, not twenty yards across in any direction. The leading troopers reached the edge almost as the bear tumbled in. One of them, a tall and powerful man named Miller, instantly dismounted and prepared to force his way in among the dwarfed willows, which were but breast-high. Among the men who had ridden up were Moore and Bates, and also the two famous scouts, Buffalo Bill—long a companion of Captain Moore,—and California Joe, Custer's faithful follower. California Joe had spent almost all his life on the plains and in the mountains, as a hunter and Indian fighter; and when he saw the trooper about to rush into the thicket he called out to him not to do so, warning him of the danger. But the man was a very reckless fellow and he answered by jeering at the old hunter for his over-caution in being afraid of a crippled bear. California Joe made no further effort to dissuade him, remarking quietly: "Very well, sonny, go in; it's your own affair." Miller then leaped off the bank on which they stood and strode into the thicket, holding his rifle at the port. Hardly had he taken three steps when the bear rose in front of him, roaring with rage and pain. It was so close that the man had no chance to fire. Its fore-arms hung useless and as it reared unsteadily on its hind-legs, lunging forward at him, he seized it by the ears and strove to hold it back. His strength was very great, and he actually kept the huge head from his face and braced himself so that he was not overthrown; but the bear twisted its muzzle from side to side, biting and tearing the man's arms and shoulders. Another soldier jumping down slew the beast with a single bullet, and rescued his comrade; but though alive he was too badly hurt to recover and died after reaching the hospital. Buffalo Bill was given the bear-skin, and I believe he has it now.

The instances in which hunters who have rashly followed grislies into thick cover have been killed or severely mauled might be multiplied indefinitely. I have myself known of eight cases in which men have met their deaths in this manner.

It occasionally happens that a cunning old grisly will lie so close that the hunter almost steps on him; and he then rises suddenly with a loud, coughing growl and strikes down or seizes the man before the latter can fire off his rifle. More rarely a bear which is both vicious and crafty deliberately permits the hunter to approach fairly near to, or perhaps pass by, its hiding place, and then suddenly charges him with such rapidity that he has barely time for the most hurried shot. The danger in such a case is of course great.

Ordinarily, however, even in the brush, the bear's object is to slink away, not to fight, and very many are killed even under the most unfavorable circumstances without accident. If an unwounded bear thinks itself unobserved it is not apt to attack; and in thick cover it is really astonishing to see how one of these large animals can hide, and how closely it will lie when there is danger. About twelve miles below my ranch there are some large river bottoms and creek bottoms covered with a matted mass of cottonwood, box-alders, bullberry bushes, rosebushes, ash, wild plums, and other bushes. These bottoms have harbored bear ever since I first saw them; but, though often in company with a large party, I have repeatedly beaten through them, and though we must at times have been very near indeed to the game, we never so much as heard it run.

When bears are shot, as they usually must be, in open timber or on the bare mountain, the risk is very much less. Hundreds may thus be killed with comparatively little danger; yet even under these circumstances they will often charge, and sometimes make their charge good. The spice of danger, especially to a man armed with a good repeating rifle, is only enough to add zest to the chase, and the chief triumph is in outwitting the wary quarry and getting within range. Ordinarily the only excitement is in the stalk, the bear doing nothing more than keep a keen lookout and manifest the utmost anxiety to get away. As is but natural, accidents occasionally occur; yet they are usually due more to some failure in man or weapon than to the prowess of the bear. A good hunter whom I once knew, at a time when he was living in Butte, received fatal injuries from a bear he attacked in open woodland. The beast charged after the first shot, but slackened its pace on coming almost up to the man. The latter's gun jammed, and as he was endeavoring to work it he kept stepping slowly back, facing the bear which followed a few yards distant, snarling and threatening. Unfortunately while thus walking backward the man struck a dead log and fell over it, whereupon the beast instantly sprang upon him and mortally wounded him before help arrived.

On rare occasions men who are not at the time hunting it fall victims to the grisly. This is usually because they stumble on it unawares and the animal attacks them more in fear than in anger. One such case, resulting fatally, occurred near my own ranch. The man walked almost over a bear while crossing a little point of brush, in a bend of the river, and was brained with a single blow of the paw. In another instance which came to my knowledge the man escaped with a shaking up, and without even a fright. His name was Perkins, and he was out gathering huckleberries in the woods on a mountain side near Pend d'Oreille Lake. Suddenly he was sent flying head over heels, by a blow which completely knocked the breath out of his body; and so instantaneous was the whole affair that all he could ever recollect about it was getting a vague glimpse of the bear just as he was bowled over. When he came to he found himself lying some distance down the hill-side, much shaken, and without his berry pail, which had rolled a hundred yards below him, but not otherwise the worse for his misadventure; while the footprints showed that the bear, after delivering the single hurried stroke at the unwitting disturber of its day-dreams, had run off uphill as fast as it was able.

A she-bear with cubs is a proverbially dangerous beast; yet even under such conditions different grislies act in directly opposite ways. Some she-grislies, when their cubs are young, but are able to follow them about, seem always worked up to the highest pitch of anxious and jealous rage, so that they are likely to attack unprovoked any intruder or even passer-by. Others when threatened by the hunter leave their cubs to their fate without a visible qualm of any kind, and seem to think only of their own safety.

In 1882 Mr. Caspar W. Whitney, now of New York, met with a very singular adventure with a she-bear and cub. He was in Harvard when I was, but left it and, like a good many other Harvard men of that time, took to cow-punching in the West. He went on a ranch in Rio Arriba County, New Mexico, and was a keen hunter, especially fond of the chase of cougar, bear, and elk. One day while riding a stony mountain trail he saw a little grisly cub watching him from the chaparral above, and he dismounted to try to capture it; his rifle was a 40-90 Sharps. Just as he neared the cub, he heard a growl and caught a glimpse of the old she, and he at once turned uphill, and stood under some tall, quaking aspens. From this spot he fired at and wounded the she, then seventy yards off; and she charged furiously. He hit her again, but as she kept coming like a thunderbolt he climbed hastily up the aspen, dragging his gun with him, as it had a strap. When the bear reached the foot of the aspen she reared, and bit and clawed the slender trunk, shaking it for a moment, and he shot her through the eye. Off she sprang for a few yards, and then spun round a dozen times, as if dazed or partially stunned; for the bullet had not touched the brain. Then the vindictive and resolute beast came back to the tree and again reared up against it; this time to receive a bullet that dropped her lifeless. Mr. Whitney then climbed down and walked to where the cub had been sitting as a looker-on. The little animal did not move until he reached out his hand; when it suddenly struck at him like an angry cat, dived into the bushes, and was seen no more.

In the summer of 1888 an old-time trapper, named Charley Norton, while on Loon Creek, of the middle fork of the Salmon, meddled with a she and her cubs. She ran at him and with one blow of her paw almost knocked off his lower jaw; yet he recovered, and was alive when I last heard of him.

Yet the very next spring the cowboys with my own wagon on the Little Missouri roundup killed a mother bear which made but little more fight than a coyote. She had two cubs, and was surprised in the early morning on the prairie far from cover. There were eight or ten cowboys together at the time, just starting off on a long circle, and of course they all got down their ropes in a second, and putting spurs to their fiery little horses started toward the bears at a run, shouting and swinging their loops round their heads. For a moment the old she tried to bluster and made a half-hearted threat of charging; but her courage failed before the rapid onslaught of her yelling, rope-swinging assailants; and she took to her heels and galloped off, leaving the cubs to shift for themselves. The cowboys were close behind, however, and after half a mile's run she bolted into a shallow cave or hole in the side of a butte, where she stayed cowering and growling, until one of the men leaped off his horse, ran up to the edge of the hole, and killed her with a single bullet from his revolver, fired so close that the powder burned her hair. The unfortunate cubs were roped, and then so dragged about that they were speedily killed instead of being brought alive to camp, as ought to have been done.

In the cases mentioned above the grisly attacked only after having been itself assailed, or because it feared an assault, for itself or for its young. In the old days, however, it may almost be said that a grisly was more apt to attack than to flee. Lewis and Clark and the early explorers who immediately succeeded them, as well as the first hunters and trappers, the "Rocky Mountain men" of the early decades of the present century, were repeatedly assailed in this manner; and not a few of the bear hunters of that period found that it was unnecessary to take much trouble about approaching their quarry, as the grisly was usually prompt to accept the challenge and to advance of its own accord, as soon as it discovered the foe. All this is changed now. Yet even at the present day an occasional vicious old bear may be found, in some far-off and little-trod fastness, which still keeps up the former habit of its kind. All old hunters have tales of this sort to relate, the prowess, cunning, strength, and ferocity of the grisly being favorite topics for camp fire talk throughout the Rockies; but in most cases it is not safe to accept these stories without careful sifting.

Still, it is just as unsafe to reject them all. One of my own cowboys was once attacked by a grisly, seemingly in pure wantonness. He was riding up a creek bottom, and had just passed a clump of rose and bullberry bushes when his horse gave such a leap as almost to unseat him, and then darted madly forward. Turning round in the saddle, to his utter astonishment he saw a large bear galloping after him, at the horse's heels. For a few jumps the race was close, then the horse drew away and the bear wheeled and went into a thicket of wild plums. The amazed and indignant cowboy, as soon as he could rein in his steed, drew his revolver and rode back to and around the thicket, endeavoring to provoke his late pursuer to come out and try conclusions on more equal terms; but prudent Ephraim had apparently repented of his freak of ferocious bravado, and declined to leave the secure shelter of the jungle.

Other attacks are of a much more explicable nature. Mr. Huffman, the photographer of Miles City, informed me that once when butchering some slaughtered elk he was charged twice by a she-bear and two well-grown cubs. This was a piece of sheer bullying, undertaken solely with the purpose of driving away the man and feasting on the carcasses; for in each charge the three bears, after advancing with much blustering, roaring, and growling, halted just before coming to close quarters. In another instance a gentleman I once knew, a Mr. S. Carr, was charged by a grisly from mere ill temper at being disturbed at meal-time. The man was riding up a valley; and the bear was at an elk carcass, near a clump of firs. As soon as it became aware of the approach of the horseman, while he was yet over a hundred yards distant, it jumped on the carcass, looked at him a moment, and then ran straight for him. There was no particular reason why it should have charged, for it was fat and in good trim, though when killed its head showed scars made by the teeth of rival grislies. Apparently it had been living so well, principally on flesh, that it had become quarrelsome; and perhaps its not over sweet disposition had been soured by combats with others of its own kind. In yet another case, a grisly charged with even less excuse. An old trapper, from whom I occasionally bought fur, was toiling up a mountain pass when he spied a big bear sitting on his haunches on the hillside above. The trapper shouted and waved his cap; whereupon, to his amazement, the bear uttered a loud "wough" and charged straight down on him— only to fall a victim to misplaced boldness.

I am even inclined to think that there have been wholly exceptional occasions when a grisly has attacked a man with the deliberate purpose of making a meal of him; when, in other words, it has started on the career of a man-eater. At least, on any other theory I find it difficult to account for an attack which once came to my knowledge. I was at Sand Point, on Pend d'Oreille Lake, and met some French and Méti trappers, then in town with their bales of beaver, otter, and sable. One of them, who gave his name as Baptiste Lamoche, had his head twisted over to one side, the result of the bite of a bear. When the accident occurred he was out on a trapping trip with two companions. They had pitched camp right on the shore of a cove in a little lake, and his comrades were off fishing in a dugout or pirogue. He himself was sitting near the shore, by a little lean-to, watching some beaver meat which was sizzling over the dying embers. Suddenly, and without warning, a great bear, which had crept silently up beneath the shadows of the tall evergreens, rushed at him, with a guttural roar, and seized him before he could rise to his feet. It grasped him with its jaws at the junction of the neck and shoulder, making the teeth meet through bone, sinew, and muscle; and turning, tracked off toward the forest, dragging with it the helpless and paralyzed victim. Luckily the two men in the canoe had just paddled round the point, in sight of, and close to, camp. The man in the bow, seeing the plight of their comrade, seized his rifle and fired at the bear. The bullet went through the beast's lungs, and it forthwith dropped its prey, and running off some two hundred yards, lay down on its side and died. The rescued man recovered full health and strength, but never again carried his head straight.

Old hunters and mountain men tell many stories, not only of malicious grislies thus attacking men in camp, but also of their even dogging the footsteps of some solitary hunter and killing him when the favorable opportunity occurs. Most of these tales are mere fables; but it is possible that in altogether exceptional instances they rest on a foundation of fact. One old hunter whom I knew told me such a story. He was a truthful old fellow, and there was no doubt that he believed what he said, and that his companion was actually killed by a bear; but it is probable that he was mistaken in reading the signs of his comrade's fate, and that the latter was not dogged by the bear at all, but stumbled on him and was slain in the surprise of the moment.

At any rate, cases of wanton assaults by grislies are altogether out of the common. The ordinary hunter may live out his whole life in the wilderness and never know aught of a bear attacking a man unprovoked; and the great majority of bears are shot under circumstances of no special excitement, as they either make no fight at all, or, if they do fight, are killed before there is any risk of their doing damage. If surprised on the plains, at some distance from timber or from badly broken ground, it is no uncommon feat for a single horseman to kill them with a revolver. Twice of late years it has been performed in the neighborhood of my ranch. In both instances the men were not hunters out after game, but simply cowboys, riding over the range in early morning in pursuance of their ordinary duties among the cattle. I knew both men and have worked with them on the round-up. Like most cowboys they carried 44-calibre Colt revolvers, and were accustomed to and fairly expert in their use, and they were mounted on ordinary cow-ponies — quick, wiry, plucky little beasts. In one case the bear was seen from quite a distance, lounging across a broad tableland. The cowboy, by taking advantage of a winding and rather shallow coulie, got quite close to him. He then scrambled out of the coulie, put spurs to his pony, and raced up to within fifty yards of the astonished bear ere the latter quite understood what it was that was running at him through the gray dawn. He made no attempt at fight, but ran at top speed toward a clump of brush not far off at the head of a creek. Before he could reach it, however, the galloping horseman was alongside, and fired three shots into his broad back. He did not turn, but ran on into the bushes and then fell over and died.

In the other case the cowboy, a Texan, was mounted on a good cutting pony, a spirited, handy, agile little animal, but excitable, and with a habit of dancing, which rendered it difficult to shoot from its back. The man was with the round-up wagon, and had been sent off by himself to make a circle through some low, barren buttes, where it was not thought more than a few head of stock would be found. On rounding the corner of a small washout he almost ran over a bear which was feeding on the carcass of a steer that had died in an alkali hole. After a moment of stunned surprise the bear hurled himself at the intruder with furious impetuosity; while the cowboy, wheeling his horse on its haunches and dashing in the spurs, carried it just clear of his assailant's headlong rush. After a few springs he reined in and once more wheeled half round, having drawn his revolver, only to find the bear again charging and almost on him. This time he fired into it, near the joining of the neck and shoulder, the bullet going downward into the chest hollow; and again by a quick dash to one side he just avoided the rush of the beast and the sweep of its mighty forepaw. The bear then halted for a minute, and he rode close by it at a run, firing a couple of shots, which brought on another resolute charge. The ground was quite rugged and broken, but his pony was as quick on its feet as a cat, and never stumbled, even when going at full speed to avoid the bear's first mad rushes. It speedily became so excited, however, as to render it almost impossible for the rider to take aim. Sometimes he would come up close to the bear and wait for it to charge, which it would do, first at a trot, or rather rack, and then at a lumbering but swift gallop; and he would fire one or two shots before being forced to run. At other times, if the bear stood still in a good place, he would run by it, firing as he rode. He spent many cartridges, and though most of them were wasted, occasionally a bullet went home. The bear fought with the most savage courage, champing its bloody jaws, roaring with rage, and looking the very incarnation of evil fury. For some minutes it made no effort to flee, either charging or standing at bay. Then it began to move slowly toward a patch of ash and wild plums in the head of a coulie, some distance off. Its pursuer rode after it, and when close enough would push by it and fire, while the bear would spin quickly round and charge as fiercely as ever, though evidently beginning to grow weak. At last, when still a couple of hundred yards from cover, the man found he had used up all his cartridges, and then merely followed at a safe distance. The bear no longer paid heed to him, but walked slowly forward, swaying its great head from side to side, while the blood streamed from between its half-opened jaws. On reaching the cover he could tell by the waving of the bushes that it walked to the middle and then halted. A few minutes afterward some of the other cowboys rode up, having been attracted by the incessant firing. They surrounded the thicket, firing and throwing stones into the bushes. Finally, as nothing moved, they ventured in and found the indomitable grisly warrior lying dead.

Cowboys delight in nothing so much as the chance to show their skill as riders and ropers; and they always try to ride down and rope any wild animal they come across in favorable ground and close enough up. If a party of them meets a bear in the open they have great fun; and the struggle between the shouting, galloping rough-riders and their shaggy quarry is full of wild excitement and not unaccompanied by danger. The bear often throws the noose from his head so rapidly that it is a difficult matter to catch him; and his frequent charges scatter his tormentors in every direction, while the horses become wild with fright over the roaring, bristling beast—for horses seem to dread a bear more than any other animal. If the bear cannot reach cover, however, his fate is sealed. Sooner or later, the noose tightens over one leg, or perchance over the neck and forepaw, and as the rope straightens with a "pluck," the horse braces itself desperately and the bear tumbles over. Whether he regains his feet or not the cowboy keeps the rope taut; soon another noose tightens over a leg, and the bear is speedily rendered helpless.

I have known of these feats being performed several times in northern Wyoming, although never in the immediate neighborhood of my ranch. Mr. Archibald Roger's cowhands have in this manner caught several bears, on or near his ranch on the Gray Bull, which flows into the Bighorn; and those of Mr. G. B. Grinnell have also occasionally done so. Any set of moderately good ropers and riders, who are accustomed to back one another up and act together, can accomplish the feat if they have smooth ground and plenty of room. It is, however, indeed a feat of skill and daring for a single man; and yet I have known of more than one instance in which it has been accomplished by some reckless knight of the rope and the saddle. One such occurred in 1887 on the Flathead

Reservation, the hero being a half-breed; and another in 1890 at the mouth of the Bighorn, where a cowboy roped, bound, and killed a large bear single-handed.

My friend General "Red" Jackson, of Bellemeade, in the pleasant mid-county of Tennessee, once did a feat which casts into the shade even the feats of the men of the lariat. General Jackson, who afterward became one of the ablest and most renowned of the Confederate cavalry leaders, was at the time a young officer in the Mounted Rifle Regiment, now known as the 3d United States Cavalry. It was some years before the Civil War, and the regiment was on duty in the Southwest, then the debatable land of Comanche and Apache. While on a scout after hostile Indians, the troops in their march roused a large grisly which sped off across the plain in front of them. Strict orders had been issued against firing at game, because of the nearness of the Indians. Young Jackson was a man of great strength, a keen swordsman, who always kept the finest edge on his blade, and he was on a swift and mettled Kentucky horse, which luckily had but one eye. Riding at full speed he soon overtook the quarry. As the horse hoofs sounded nearer, the grim bear ceased its flight, and whirling round stood at bay, raising itself on its hind-legs and threatening its pursuer with bared fangs and spread claws. Carefully riding his horse so that its blind side should be toward the monster, the cavalryman swept by at a run, handling his steed with such daring skill that he just cleared the blow of the dreaded forepaw, while with one mighty sabre stroke he cleft the bear's skull, slaying the grinning beast as it stood upright.

CHAPTER V

THE COUGAR

No animal of the chase is so difficult to kill by fair still-hunting as the cougar — that beast of many names, known in the East as panther and painter, in the West as mountain lion, in the Southwest as Mexican lion, and in the southern continent as lion and puma.

Without hounds its pursuit is so uncertain that from the still-hunter's standpoint it hardly deserves to rank as game at all — though, by the way, it is itself a more skilful still-hunter than any human rival. It prefers to move abroad by night or at dusk; and in the daytime usually lies hid in some cave or tangled thicket where it is absolutely impossible even to stumble on it by chance. It is a beast of stealth and rapine, its great velvet paws never make a sound, and it is always on the watch whether for prey or for enemies, while it rarely leaves shelter even when it thinks itself safe. Its soft, leisurely movements and uniformity of color make it difficult to discover at best, and its extreme watchfulness helps it; but it is the cougar's reluctance to leave cover at any time, its habit of slinking off through the brush, instead of running in the open, when startled, and the way in which it lies motionless in its lair even when a man is within twenty yards, that render it so difficult to still-hunt.

In fact it is next to impossible with any hope of success regularly to hunt the cougar without dogs or bait. Most cougars that are killed by still-hunters are shot by accident while the man is after other game. This has been my own experience. Although not common, cougars are found near my ranch, where the ground is peculiarly favorable for the solitary rifleman; and for ten years I have, off and on, devoted a day or two to their pursuit; but never successfully. One December a large cougar took up his abode on a densely wooded bottom two miles above the ranch house. I did not discover his existence until I went there one evening to kill a deer, and found that he had driven all the deer off the bottom, having killed several, as well as a young heifer. Snow was falling at the time, but the storm was evidently almost over; the leaves were all off the trees and bushes; and I felt that next day there would be such a chance to follow the cougar as fate rarely offered. In the morning by dawn I was at the bottom, and speedily found his trail. Following it I came across his bed, among some cedars in a dark, steep gorge, where the buttes bordered the bottom. He had evidently just left it, and I followed his tracks all day. But I never caught a glimpse of him, and late in the afternoon I trudged wearily homeward. When I went out next morning I found that as soon as I abandoned the chase, my quarry, according to the uncanny habit sometimes displayed by his kind, coolly turned likewise, and deliberately dogged my footsteps to within a mile of the ranch house; his round footprints being as clear as writing in the snow.

This was the best chance of the kind that I ever had; but again and again I have found fresh signs of cougar, such as a lair which they had just left, game they had killed, or one of our venison caches which they had robbed, and have hunted for them all day without success. My failures were doubtless due in part to various shortcomings in hunter's-craft on my own part; but equally without doubt they were mainly due to the quarry's wariness and its sneaking ways.

I have seen a wild cougar alive but twice, and both times by chance. On one occasion one of my men, Merrifield, and I surprised one eating a skunk in a bullberry patch; and by our own bungling frightened it away from its unsavory repast without getting a shot.

On the other occasion luck befriended me. I was with a pack train in the Rockies, and one day, feeling lazy, and as we had no meat in camp, I determined to try for deer by lying in wait beside a recently traveled game trail. The spot I chose was a steep, pine-clad slope leading down to a little mountain lake. I hid behind a breastwork of rotten logs, with a few young evergreens in front— an excellent ambush. A broad game trail slanted down the hill directly past me. I lay perfectly quiet for about an hour, listening to the murmur of the pine forests, and the occasional call of a jay or woodpecker, and gazing eagerly along the trail in the waning light of the late afternoon. Suddenly, without noise or warning of any kind, a cougar stood in the trail before me. The unlooked-for and unheralded approach of the beast was fairly ghost-like. With its head lower than its shoulders, and its long tail twitching, it slouched down the path, treading as softly as a kitten. I waited until it had passed and then fired into the short ribs, the bullet ranging forward. Throwing its tail up in the air, and giving a bound, the cougar galloped off over a slight ridge. But it did not go far; within a hundred yards I found it stretched on its side, its jaws still working convulsively.

The true way to hunt the cougar is to follow it with dogs. If the chase is conducted in this fashion it is very exciting, and resembles on a larger scale the ordinary method of hunting the wildcat or small lynx, as practiced by the sport-loving planters of the southern states. With a very little training, hounds readily and eagerly pursue the cougar, showing in this kind of chase none of the fear and disgust they are so prone to exhibit when put on the trail of the certainly no more dangerous wolf. The cougar, when the hounds are on its track, at first runs, but when hard-pressed takes to a tree, or possibly comes to bay in thick cover. Its attention is then so taken up with the hounds that it can usually be approached and shot without much difficulty; though some cougars break bay when the hunters come near, and again make off, when they can only be stopped by many large and fierce hounds. Hounds are often killed in these fights; and if hungry a cougar will pounce on any dog for food; yet, as I have elsewhere related, I know of one instance in which a small pack of big, savage hounds killed a cougar unassisted. General Wade Hampton, who with horse and hound has been the mightiest hunter America has ever seen, informs me that he has killed with his pack some sixteen cougars, during the fifty years he has hunted in South Carolina and Mississippi. I believe they were all killed in the latter state. General Hampton's hunting has been chiefly for bear and deer, though his pack also follows the lynx and the gray fox; and, of course, if good fortune throws either a wolf or a cougar in his way it is followed as the game of all others. All the cougars he killed were either treed or brought to bay in a canebrake by the hounds; and they often handled the pack very roughly in the death struggle. He found them much more dangerous antagonists than the black bear when assailed with the hunting knife, a weapon of which he was very fond. However, if his pack had held a few very large, savage dogs, put in purely for fighting when the quarry was at bay, I think the danger would have been minimized.

General Hampton followed his game on horseback; but in following the cougar with dogs this is by no means always necessary. Thus Colonel Cecil Clay, of Washington, killed a cougar in West Virginia, on foot with only three or four hounds. The dogs took the cold trail, and he had to run many miles over the rough, forest-clad mountains after them. Finally they drove the cougar up a tree; where he found it, standing among the branches, in a half-erect position, its hind-feet on one limb and its fore-feet on another, while it glared down at the dogs, and switched its tail from side to side. He shot it through both shoulders, and down it came in a heap, whereupon the dogs jumped in and worried it, for its fore-legs were useless, though it managed to catch one dog in its jaws and bite him severely.

A wholly exceptional instance of the kind was related to me by my old hunting friend Willis. In his youth, in southwest Missouri, he knew a half-witted "poor white" who was very fond of hunting coons. He hunted at night, armed with an axe, and accompanied by his dog Penny, a large, savage, half-starved cur. One dark night the dog treed an animal which he could not see; so he cut down the tree, and immediately Penny jumped in and grabbed the beast. The man sung out "Hold on, Penny," seeing that the dog had seized some large, wild animal; the next moment the brute knocked the dog endways, and at the same instant the man split open its head with the axe. Great was his astonishment, and greater still the astonishment of the neighbors next day, when it was found that he had actually killed a cougar. These great cats often take to trees in a perfectly foolish manner. My friend, the hunter Woody, in all his thirty years' experience in the wilds never killed but one cougar. He was lying out in camp with two dogs at the time; it was about midnight, the fire was out, and the night was pitch-black. He was roused by the furious barking of his two dogs, who had charged into the gloom, and were apparently baying at something in a tree close by. He kindled the fire, and to his astonishment found the thing in the tree to be a cougar. Coming close underneath he shot it with his revolver; thereupon it leaped down, ran some forty yards, and climbed up another tree, where it died among the branches.

If cowboys come across a cougar in open ground they invariably chase and try to rope it—as indeed they do with any wild animal. I have known several instances of cougars being roped in this way; in one the animal was brought into camp alive by two strapping cowpunchers.

The cougar sometimes stalks its prey, and sometimes lies in wait for it beside a game-trail or drinking pool—very rarely indeed does it crouch on the limb of a tree. When excited by the presence of game it is sometimes very bold. Willis once fired at some big-horn sheep, on a steep mountain-side; he missed, and immediately after his shot a cougar made a dash into the midst of the flying band, hoping to secure a victim. The cougar roams over long distances, and often changes its hunting ground, perhaps remaining in one place two or three months, until the game is exhausted, and then shifting to another. When it does not lie in wait it usually spends most of the night, winter and summer, in prowling restlessly around the places where it thinks it may come across prey, and it will patiently follow an animal's trail. There is no kind of game, save the full-grown grisly and buffalo, which it does not at times assail and master. It readily snaps up grisly cubs or buffalo calves; and in at least one instance, I have known of it springing on, slaying, and eating a full-grown wolf. I presume the latter was taken by surprise. On the other hand, the cougar itself has to fear the big timber wolves when maddened by the winter hunger and gathered in small parties; while a large grisly would of course be an overmatch for it twice over, though its superior agility puts it beyond the grisly's power to harm it, unless by some unlucky chance taken in a cave. Nor could a cougar overcome a bull moose, or a bull elk either, if the latter's horns were grown, save by taking it unawares. By choice, with such big game, its victims are the cows and young. The prong-horn rarely comes within reach of its spring; but it is the dreaded enemy of big-horn, white goat, and every kind of deer, while it also preys on all the smaller beasts, such as foxes, coons, rabbits, beavers, and even gophers, rats, and mice. It sometimes makes a thorny meal of the porcupine, and if sufficiently hungry attacks and eats its smaller cousin the lynx. It is not a brave animal; nor does it run its prey down in open chase. It always makes its attacks by stealth, and if possible from behind, and relies on two or three tremendous springs to bring it on the doomed creature's back. It uses its claws as well as its teeth in holding and killing the prey. If possible it always seizes a large animal by the throat, whereas the wolf's point of attack is more often the haunch or flank. Small deer or sheep it will often knock over and kill, merely using its big paws; sometimes it breaks their necks. It has a small head compared to the jaguar, and its bite is much less dangerous. Hence, as compared to its larger and bolder relative, it places more trust in its claws and less in its teeth.

Though the cougar prefers woodland, it is not necessarily a beast of the dense forests only; for it is found in all the plains country, living in the scanty timber belts which fringe the streams,

or among the patches of brush in the Bad Lands. The persecution
of hunters, however, always tends to drive it into the most thickly
wooded and broken fastnesses of the mountains. The she has
from one to three kittens, brought forth in a cave or a secluded
lair, under a dead log or in very thick brush. It is said that the old
hes kill the small male kittens when they get a chance. They certainly at times during the breeding season fight desperately
among themselves. Cougars are very solitary beasts; it is rare to see
more than one at a time, and then only a mother and young, or a
mated male and female. While she has kittens, the mother is dou-
bly destructive to game. The young begin to kill for themselves
very early. The first fall, after they are born, they attack large
game, and from ignorance are bolder in making their attacks than
their parents; but they are clumsy and often let the prey escape.
Like all cats, cougars are comparatively easy to trap, much more so
than beasts of the dog kind, such as the fox and wolf.

They are silent animals; but old hunters say that at mating time
the males call loudly, while the females have a very distinct answer.
They are also sometimes noisy at other seasons. I am not sure that
I ever heard one; but one night, while camped in a heavily timbered coulie near Kildeer Mountains, where, as their footprints
showed, the beasts were plentiful, I twice heard a loud, wailing
scream ringing through the impenetrable gloom which shrouded
the hills around us. My companion, an old plainsman, said that
this was the cry of the cougar prowling for its prey. Certainly no
man could well listen to a stranger and wilder sound.

Ordinarily the rifleman is in no danger from a hunted cougar;
the beast's one idea seems to be flight, and even if its assailant is
very close, it rarely charges if there is any chance for escape. Yet
there are occasions when it will show fight. In the spring of 1890,
a man with whom I had more than once worked on the round-up—
though I never knew his name—was badly mauled by a cougar
near my ranch. He was hunting with a companion and they unex-
pectedly came on the cougar on a shelf of sandstone above their
heads, only some ten feet off. It sprang down on the man, man-

gled him with teeth and claws for a moment, and then ran away. Another man I knew, a hunter named Ed Smith, who had a small ranch near Helena, was once charged by a wounded cougar; he received a couple of deep scratches, but was not seriously hurt.

Many old frontiersmen tell tales of the cougar's occasionally itself making the attack, and dogging to his death some unfortunate wayfarer. Many others laugh such tales to scorn. It is certain that if such attacks occur they are altogether exceptional, being indeed of such extreme rarity that they may be entirely disregarded in practice. I should have no more hesitation in sleeping out in a wood where there were cougars, or walking through it after nightfall, than I should have if the cougars were tomcats.

Yet it is foolish to deny that in exceptional instances attacks may occur. Cougars vary wonderfully in size, and no less in temper. Indeed I think that by nature they are as ferocious and bloodthirsty as they are cowardly; and that their habit of sometimes dogging wayfarers for miles is due to a desire for bloodshed which they lack the courage to realize. In the old days, when all wild beasts were less shy than at present, there was more danger from the cougar; and this was especially true in the dark canebrakes of some of the southern states, where the man a cougar was most likely to encounter was a nearly naked and unarmed negro. General Hampton tells me that near his Mississippi plantation, many years ago, a negro who was one of a gang engaged in building a railroad through low and wet ground was waylaid and killed by a cougar late one night as he was walking alone through the swamp.

I knew two men in Missoula who were once attacked by cougars in a very curious manner. It was in January, and they were walking home through the snow after a hunt, each carrying on his back the saddle, haunches, and hide of a deer he had slain. Just at dusk, as they were passing through a narrow ravine, the man in front heard his partner utter a sudden loud call for help. Turning, he was dumfounded to see the man lying on his face in the snow, with a cougar which had evidently just knocked him down standing over him, grasping the deer meat; while another cougar was galloping up to assist. Swinging his rifle round he shot the first one in the brain, and it dropped motionless, whereat the second halted, wheeled, and bounded into the woods. His companion was not in the least hurt or even frightened. The cougars were not full grown, but young of the year.

Now in this case I do not believe the beasts had any real intention of attacking the men. They were young animals, bold, stupid, and very hungry. The smell of the raw meat excited them beyond control, and they probably could not make out clearly what the men were, as they walked bent under their burdens, with the deer skins on their backs. Evidently the cougars were only trying to get at the venison.

In 1886 a cougar killed an Indian near Flathead Lake. Two Indians were hunting together on horseback when they came on the cougar. It fell at once to their shots, and they dismounted and ran toward it. Just as they reached it, it came to, and seized one, killing him instantly with a couple of savage bites in the throat and chest; it then raced after the other, and, as he sprung on his horse, struck him across the buttocks, inflicting a deep but not dangerous scratch. I saw this survivor a year later. He evinced great reluctance to talk of the event, and insisted that the thing which had slain his companion was not really a cougar at all, but a devil.

A she-cougar does not often attempt to avenge the loss of her young, but sometimes she does. A remarkable instance of the kind happened to my friend, Professor John Bach McMaster, in 1875. He was camped near the head of Green River, Wyoming. One afternoon he found a couple of cougar kittens, and took them into camp; they were clumsy, playful, friendly little creatures. The next afternoon he remained in camp with the cook. Happening to look up he suddenly spied the mother cougar running noiselessly down on them, her eyes glaring and tail twitching. Snatching up his rifle, he killed her when she was barely twenty yards distant.

A ranchman, named Trescott, who was at one time my neighbor, told me that while he was living on a sheep-farm in the Argentine, he found pumas very common, and killed many. They were very destructive to sheep and colts, but were singularly cowardly when dealing with men. Not only did they never attack human beings, under any stress of hunger, but they made no effective resistance when brought to bay, merely scratching and cuffing like a big cat; so that, if found in a cave, it was safe to creep in and shoot them with a revolver. Jaguars, on the contrary, were very dangerous antagonists.

CHAPTER VI

A PECCARY HUNT ON THE NUECES

In the United States the peccary is only found in the southern-most corner of Texas. In April, 1892, I made a flying visit to the ranch country of this region, starting from the town of Uvalde with a Texan friend, Mr. John Moore. My trip being very hurried, I had but a couple of days to devote to hunting.

Our first halting-place was at a ranch on the Frio; a low, wooden building, of many rooms, with open galleries between them, and verandas round about. The country was in some respects like, in others strangely unlike, the northern plains with which I was so well acquainted. It was for the most part covered with a scattered growth of tough, stunted mesquite trees, not dense enough to be called a forest, and yet sufficiently close to cut off the view. It was very dry, even as compared with the northern plains. The bed of the Frio was filled with coarse gravel, and for the most part dry as a bone on the surface, the water seeping through underneath, and only appearing in occasional deep holes. These deep holes or ponds never fail, even after a year's drought; they were filled with fish. One lay quite near the ranch house, under a bold rocky bluff; at its edge grew giant cypress trees. In the hollows and by the watercourses were occasional groves of pecans, live-oaks, and elms. Strange birds hopped among the bushes; the chaparral cock — a big, handsome ground-cuckoo of remarkable habits, much given to preying on small snakes and lizards—ran over the ground with extraordinary rapidity. Beautiful swallow-tailed king-birds with rosy plumage perched on the tops of the small trees, and soared and flitted in graceful curves above them. Blackbirds of many kinds scuttled in flocks about the corrals and outbuildings around the ranches. Mockingbirds abounded, and were very noisy, singing almost all the daytime, but with their usual irritating inequality of performance, wonderfully musical and powerful snatches of song being interspersed with imitations of other bird notes and disagreeable squalling. Throughout the trip I did not hear one of them utter the beautiful love song in which they sometimes indulge at night.

The country was all under wire fence, unlike the northern regions, the pastures, however, being sometimes many miles across. When we reached the Frio ranch a herd of a thousand cattle had just been gathered, and two or three hundred beeves and young stock were being cut out to be driven northward over the trail. The cattle were worked in pens much more than in the North, and on all the ranches there were chutes with steering gates, by means of which the individuals of a herd could be dexterously shifted into various corrals. The branding of the calves was done ordinarily in one of these corrals and on foot, the calf being always roped by both fore-legs; otherwise the work of the cow-punchers was much like that of their brothers in the North. As a whole, however, they were distinctly more proficient with the rope, and at least half of them were Mexicans.

There were some bands of wild cattle living only in the densest timber of the river bottoms which were literally as wild as deer, and moreover very fierce and dangerous. The pursuit of these was exciting and hazardous in the extreme. The men who took part in it showed not only the utmost daring but the most consummate horsemanship and wonderful skill in the use of the rope, the coil being hurled with the force and precision of an iron quoit; a single man speedily overtaking, roping, throwing, and binding down the fiercest steer or bull.

There had been many peccaries, or, as the Mexicans and cow-punchers of the border usually call them, javalinas, round this ranch a few years before the date of my visit. Until 1886, or there-about, these little wild hogs were not much molested, and abounded in the dense chaparral around the lower Rio Grande. In that year, however, it was suddenly discovered that their hides had a market value, being worth four bits—that is, half a dollar—apiece; and many Mexicans and not a few shiftless Texans went into the busi-ness of hunting them as a means of livelihood. They were more easily killed than deer, and, as a result, they were speedily extermi-nated in many localities where they had formerly been numerous, and even where they were left were to be found only in greatly diminished numbers. On this particular Frio ranch the last little band had been killed nearly a year before. There were three of them, a boar and two sows, and a couple of the cowboys stumbled on them early one morning while out with a dog. After half a mile's chase the three peccaries ran into a hollow pecan tree, and one of the cowboys, dismounting, improvised a lance by tying his knife to the end of a pole, and killed them all.

Many anecdotes were related to me of what they had done in the old days when they were plentiful on the ranch. They were then usually found in parties of from twenty to thirty, feeding in the dense chaparral, the sows rejoining the herd with the young very soon after the birth of the latter, each sow usually having but one or two at a litter. At night they sometimes lay in the thickest cover, but always, where possible, preferred to house in a cave or big hollow log, one invariably remaining as a sentinel close to the mouth, looking out. If this sentinel were shot, another would almost cer-tainly take his place. They were subject to freaks of stupidity, and were pugnacious to a degree. Not only would they fight if molested, but they would often attack entirely without provocation.

Once my friend Moore himself, while out with another cowboy on horseback, was attacked in sheer wantonness by a drove of these little wild hogs. The two men were riding by a grove of live-oaks along a wood-cutter's cart track, and were assailed without a moment's warning. The little creatures completely surrounded them, cutting fiercely at the horses' legs and jumping up at the riders' feet. The men, drawing their revolvers, dashed through and were closely followed by their pursuers for three or four hundred yards, although they fired right and left with good effect. Both of the horses were badly cut. On another occasion the book-keeper of the ranch walked off to a water hole but a quarter of a mile distant, and came face to face with a peccary on a cattle trail, where the brush was thick. Instead of getting out of his way the creature charged him instantly, drove him up a small mesquite tree, and kept him there for nearly two hours, looking up at him and champing its tusks.

I spent two days hunting round this ranch but saw no peccary sign whatever, although deer were quite plentiful. Parties of wild geese and sandhill cranes occasionally flew overhead. At nightfall the poor-wills wailed everywhere through the woods, and coyotes yelped and yelled, while in the early morning the wild turkeys gobbled loudly from their roosts in the tops of the pecan trees.

Having satisfied myself that there were no javalinas left on the Frio ranch, and being nearly at the end of my holiday, I was about to abandon the effort to get any, when a passing cowman happened to mention the fact that some were still to be found on the Nueces River thirty miles or thereabout to the southward. Thither I determined to go, and next morning Moore and I started in a buggy drawn by a redoubtable horse, named Jim Swinger, which we were allowed to use because he bucked so under the saddle that nobody on the ranch could ride him. We drove six or seven hours across the dry, waterless plains. There had been a heavy frost a few days before, which had blackened the budding mesquite trees, and their twigs still showed no signs of sprouting. Occasionally we came across open spaces where there was nothing but short brown grass. In most places, however, the leafless, sprawling mesquites were scattered rather thinly over the ground, cutting off an extensive view and merely adding to the melancholy barrenness of the landscape. The road was nothing but a couple of dusty wheel-tracks; the ground was parched, and the grass cropped close by the gaunt, starved cattle. As we drove along buzzards and great hawks occasionally soared overhead. Now and then we passed lines of wild-looking, long-horned steers, and once we came on the grazing horses of a cow-outfit, just preparing to start northward over the trail to the fattening pastures. Occasionally we encountered one or two cowpunchers; either Texans, habited exactly like their brethren in the North, with broad-brimmed gray hats, blue shirts, silk neckerchiefs, and leather leggings; or else Mexicans, more gaudily dressed, and wearing peculiarly stiff, very broad-brimmed hats, with conical tops.

Toward the end of our ride we got where the ground was more fertile, and there had recently been a sprinkling of rain. Here we came across wonderful flower prairies. In one spot I kept catching glimpses through the mesquite trees of lilac stretches which I had first thought must be ponds of water. On coming nearer they proved to be acres on acres thickly covered with beautiful lilac-colored flowers. Further on we came to where broad bands of red flowers covered the ground for many furlongs; then their places were taken by yellow blossoms, elsewhere by white. Generally each band or patch of ground was covered densely by flowers of the same color, making a great vivid streak across the landscape; but in places they were mixed together, red, yellow, and purple, interspersed in patches and curving bands, carpeting the prairie in a strange, bright pattern.

Finally toward evening we reached the Nueces. Where we struck it first the bed was dry, except in occasional deep, malarial-looking pools, but a short distance below there began to be a running current. Great blue herons were stalking beside these pools, and from one we flushed a white ibis. In the woods were reddish cardinal birds, much less brilliant in plumage than the true cardinals and the scarlet tanagers; and yellow-headed titmice which had already built large domed nests.

In the valley of the Nueces itself, the brush grew thick. There were great groves of pecan trees, and evergreen live-oaks stood in many places, long, wind-shaken tufts of gray moss hanging from their limbs. Many of the trees in the wet spots were of giant size, and the whole landscape was semi-tropical in character. High on a bluff shoulder overlooking the course of the river was perched the ranch house, toward which we were bending our steps; and here we were received with the hearty hospitality characteristic of the ranch country everywhere.

The son of the ranchman, a tall, well-built young fellow, told me at once that there were peccaries in the neighborhood, and that he had himself shot one but two or three days before, and volunteered to lend us horses and pilot us to the game on the morrow, with the help of his two dogs. The last were big black curs with, as we were assured, "considerable hound" in them. One was at the time staying at the ranch house, the other was four or five miles off with a Mexican goat-herder, and it was arranged that early in the morning we should ride down to the latter place, taking the first dog with us and procuring his companion when we reached the goat-herder's house.

We started after breakfast, riding powerful cow-ponies, well trained to gallop at full speed through the dense chaparral. The big black hound slouched at our heels. We rode down the banks of the Nueces, crossing and recrossing the stream. Here and there were long, deep pools in the bed of the river, where rushes and lilies grew and huge mailed garfish swam slowly just beneath the surface of the water. Once my two companions stopped to pull a mired cow out of a slough, hauling with ropes from their saddle horns. In places there were half-dry pools, out of the regular current of the river, the water green and fetid. The trees were very tall and large. The streamers of pale gray moss hung thickly from the branches of the live-oaks, and when many trees thus draped stood close together they bore a strangely mournful and desolate look.

We finally found the queer little hut of the Mexican goat-herder in the midst of a grove of giant pecans. On the walls were nailed the skins of different beasts, raccoons, wildcats, and the tree-civet, with its ringed tail. The Mexican's brown wife and children were in the hut, but the man himself and the goats were off in the forest, and it took us three or four hours' search before we found him. Then it was nearly noon, and we lunched in his hut, a square building of split logs, with bare earth floor, and roof of clap-boards and bark. Our lunch consisted of goat's meat and *pan de mais*. The Mexican, a broad-chested man with a stolid Indian face, was evidently quite a sportsman, and had two or three half-starved hounds, besides the funny, hairless little house dogs, of which Mexicans seem so fond.

Having borrowed the javalina hound of which we were in search, we rode off in quest of our game, the two dogs trotting gaily ahead. The one which had been living at the ranch had evidently fared well, and was very fat; the other was little else but skin and bone, but as alert and knowing as any New York street-boy, with the same air of disreputable capacity. It was this hound which always did most in finding the javalinas and bringing them to bay, his companion's chief use being to make a noise and lend the moral support of his presence.

We rode away from the river on the dry uplands, where the timber, though thick, was small, consisting almost exclusively of the thorny mesquites. Mixed among them were prickly pears, standing as high as our heads on horseback, and Spanish bayonets, looking in the distance like small palms; and there were many other kinds of cactus, all with poisonous thorns. Two or three times the dogs got on an old trail and rushed off giving tongue, whereat we galloped madly after them, ducking and dodging through and among the clusters of spine-bearing trees and cactus, not without getting a considerable number of thorns in our hands and legs. It was very dry and hot. Where the javalinas live in droves in the river bottoms they often drink at the pools; but when some distance from water they seem to live quite comfortably on the prickly pear, slaking their thirst by eating its hard, juicy fibre.

At last, after several false alarms, and gallops which led to nothing, when it lacked but an hour of sundown we struck a band of five of the little wild hogs. They were running off through the mesquites with a peculiar hopping or bounding motion, and we all, dogs and men, tore after them instantly.

Peccaries are very fast for a few hundred yards, but speedily tire, lose their wind, and come to bay. Almost immediately one of these, a sow, as it turned out, wheeled and charged at Moore as he passed, Moore never seeing her but keeping on after another. The sow then stopped and stood still, chattering her teeth savagely, and I jumped off my horse and dropped her dead with a shot in the spine over the shoulders. Moore meanwhile had dashed off after his pig in one direction, and killed the little beast with a shot from the saddle when it had come to bay, turning and going straight at him. Two of the peccaries got off; the remaining one, a rather large boar, was followed by the two dogs, and as soon as I had killed the sow I leaped again on my horse and made after them, guided by the yelping and baying. In less than a quarter of a mile they were on his haunches, and he wheeled and stood under a bush, charging at them when they came near him, and once catching one, inflicting an ugly cut. All the while his teeth kept going like castanets, with a rapid champing sound. I ran up close and killed him by a shot through the backbone where it joined the neck. His tusks were fine.

The few minutes' chase on horseback was great fun, and there was a certain excitement in seeing the fierce little creatures come to bay; but the true way to kill these peccaries would be with the spear. They could often be speared on horseback, and where this was impossible, by using dogs to bring them to bay they could readily be killed on foot; though, as they are very active, absolutely fearless, and inflict a most formidable bite, it would usually be safest to have two men go at one together. Peccaries are not difficult beasts to kill, because their short wind and their pugnacity make them come to bay before hounds so quickly. Two or three good dogs can bring to a halt a herd of considerable size. They then all stand in a bunch, or else with their sterns against a bank, chattering their teeth at their antagonists When angry and at bay, they get their legs close together, their shoulders high, and their bristles all ruffled and look the very incarnation of anger, and they fight with reckless indifference to the very last. Hunters usually treat them with a certain amount of caution; but, as a matter of fact, I know of but one case where a man was hurt by them. He had shot at and wounded one, was charged both by it and by its two companions, and started to climb a tree; but as he drew himself from the ground, one sprang at him and bit him through the calf, inflicting a very severe wound. I have known of several cases of horses being cut, however, and dogs are very commonly killed. Indeed, a dog new to the business is almost certain to get very badly scarred, and no dog that hunts steadily can escape without some injury. If it runs in right at the heads of the animals, the probabilities are that it will get killed; and, as a rule, even two good-sized hounds can not kill a peccary, though it is no larger than either of them. However, a wary, resolute, hard-biting dog of good size speedily gets accustomed to the chase, and can kill a peccary single-handed, seizing it from behind and worrying it to death, or watching its chance and grabbing it by the back of the neck where it joins the head.

Peccaries have delicately molded short legs, and their feet are small, the tracks looking peculiarly dainty in consequence. Hence, they do not swim well, though they take to the water if necessary. They feed on roots, prickly pears, nuts, insects, lizards, etc. They usually keep entirely separate from the droves of half-wild swine that are so often found in the same neighborhoods; but in one case, on this very ranch where I was staying, a peccary deliberately joined a party of nine pigs and associated with them. When the owner of the pigs came up to them one day the peccary manifested great suspicion at his presence, and finally sidled close up and threatened to attack him, so that he had to shoot it. The ranchman's son told me that he had never but once had a peccary assail him unprovoked, and even in this case it was his dog that was the object of attack, the peccary rushing out at it as it followed him home one evening through the chaparral. Even around this ranch the peccaries had very greatly decreased in numbers, and the survivors were learning some caution. In the old days it had been no uncommon thing for a big band to attack, entirely of their own accord, and keep a hunter up a tree for hours at a time.

CHAPTER VII

HUNTING WITH HOUNDS

In hunting American big game with hounds, several entirely distinct methods are pursued. The true wilderness hunters, the men who in the early days lived alone in, or moved in parties through, the Indian-haunted solitudes, like their successors of to-day, rarely made use of a pack of hounds, and, as a rule, did not use dogs at all. In the Eastern forests occasionally an old-time hunter would own one or two track-hounds, slow, with a good nose, intelligent and obedient, of use mainly in following wounded game. Some Rocky Mountain hunters nowadays employ the same kind of a dog, but the old-time trappers of the great plains and the Rockies led such wandering lives of peril and hardship that they could not readily take dogs with them. The hunters of the Alleghanies and the Adirondacks have, however, always used hounds to drive deer, killing the animal in the water or at a runway.

As soon, however, as the old wilderness hunter type passes away, hounds come into use among his successors, the rough border settlers of the backwoods and the plains. Every such settler is apt to have four or five large mongrel dogs with hound blood in them, which serve to drive off beasts of prey from the sheepfold and cattle-shed, and are also used, when the occasion suits, in regular hunting, whether after bear or deer.

Many of the Southern planters have always kept packs of fox-hounds, which are used in the chase, not only of the gray and the red fox, but also of the deer, the black bear, and the wildcat. The fox the dogs themselves run down and kill, but as a rule in this kind of hunting, when after deer, bear, or even wildcat, the hunters carry guns with them on their horses, and endeavor either to get a shot at the fleeing animal by hard and dexterous riding, or else to kill the cat when treed, or the bear when it comes to bay. Such hunting is great sport.

Killing driven game by lying in wait for it to pass is the very poorest kind of sport that can be called legitimate. This is the way the deer is usually killed with hounds in the East. In the North the red fox is often killed in somewhat the same manner, being followed by a slow hound and shot at as he circles before the dog. Although this kind of fox-hunting is inferior to hunting on horseback, it nevertheless has its merits, as the man must walk and run well, shoot with some accuracy, and show considerable knowledge both of the country and of the habits of the game.

During the last score of years an entirely different type of dog from the fox-hound has firmly established itself in the field of American sport. This is the greyhound, whether the smooth-haired, or the rough-coated Scotch deer-hound. For half a century the army officers posted in the far West have occasionally had greyhounds with them, using the dogs to course jack-rabbit, coyote, and sometimes deer, antelope, and gray wolf. Many of them were devoted to this sport, — General Custer, for instance. I have myself hunted with many of the descendants of Custer's hounds. In the early 70s the ranchmen of the great plains themselves began to keep greyhounds for coursing (as indeed they had already been used for a considerable time in California, after the Pacific Coast jack-rabbit), and the sport speedily assumed large proportions and a permanent form. Nowadays the ranchmen of the cattle country not only use their greyhounds after the jack-rabbit, but also after every other kind of game animal to be found there, the antelope and coyote being especial favorites. Many ranchmen soon grew to own fine packs, coursing being the sport of all sports for the plains. In Texas the wild turkey was frequently an object of the chase, and wherever the locality enabled deer to be followed in the open, as, for instance, in the Indian territory, and in many places in the neighborhood of the large plains rivers, the whitetail was a favorite quarry, the hunters striving to surprise it in the early morning when feeding on the prairie.

I have myself generally coursed with scratch packs, including perhaps a couple of greyhounds, a wire-haired deer-hound, and two or three long-legged mongrels. However, we generally had at least one very fast and savage dog—a strike dog—in each pack, and the others were of assistance in turning the game, sometimes in tiring it, and usually in helping to finish it at the worry. With such packs I have had many a wildly exciting ride over the great grassy plains lying near the Little Missouri and the Knife and Heart Rivers. Usually our proceedings on such a hunt were perfectly simple. We started on horseback and when reaching favorable ground beat across it in a long scattered line of men and dogs. Anything that we put up, from a fox to a coyote or a prong-buck, was fair game, and was instantly followed at full speed. The animals we most frequently killed were jack-rabbits. They always gave good runs, though like other game they differed much individually in speed. The foxes did not run so well, and whether they were the little swift, or the big red prairie fox, they were speedily snapped up if the dogs had a fair showing. Once our dogs roused a blacktail buck close up out of a brush coulie where the ground was moderately smooth, and after a headlong chase of a mile they ran into him, threw him and killed him before he could rise. (His stiff-legged bounds sent him along at a tremendous pace at first, but he seemed to tire rather easily.) On two or three occasions we killed whitetail deer, and several times antelope. Usually, however, the antelopes escaped. The bucks sometimes made a good fight, but generally they were seized while running, some dogs catching by the throat, others by the shoulders, and others again by the flank just in front of the hind-leg. Wherever the hold was obtained, if the dog made his spring cleverly, the buck was sure to come down with a crash, and if the other dogs were any-where near he was probably killed before he could rise, although not infrequently the dogs themselves were more or less scratched in the contests. Some greyhounds, even of high breeding, proved absolutely useless from timidity, being afraid to take hold; but if they got accustomed to the chase, being worked with old dogs, and had any pluck at all, they proved singularly fearless. A big ninety-pound greyhound or Scotch deer-hound is a very formidable fighting dog; I saw one whip a big mastiff in short order, his wonderful agility being of more account than his adversary's superior weight.

The proper way to course, however, is to take the dogs out in a wagon and drive them thus until the game is seen. This pre-vents their being tired out. In my own hunting, most of the ante-lope aroused got away, the dogs being jaded when the chase began. But really fine greyhounds, accustomed to work together and to hunt this species of game, will usually render a good account of a prong-buck if two or three are slipped at once, fresh, and within a moderate distance.

Although most Westerners take more kindly to the rifle, now and then one is found who is a devotee of the hound. Such a one was an old Missourian, who may be called Mr. Cowley, whom I knew when he was living on a ranch in North Dakota, west of the Missouri. Mr. Cowley was a primitive person, of much nerve, which he showed not only in the hunting field but in the startling politi-cal conventions of the place and period. He was quite well off; but he was above the niceties of personal vanity. His hunting garb was that in which he also paid his rare formal calls — calls throughout which he always preserved the gravity of an Indian, though having a disconcerting way of suddenly tip-toeing across the room to some unfamiliar object, such as a peacock screen or a vase, feeling it gently with one forefinger, and returning with noiseless gait to his chair, unmoved and making no comment. On the morning of a hunt he would always appear on a stout horse, clad in a long linen duster, a huge club in his hand, and his trousers working half-way up his legs. He hunted everything on all possible occasions; and he never under any circumstances shot an animal that the dogs could kill. When a skunk got into his house, with the direful stupidity of its perverse kind, he turned the hounds on it; a manifestation of sporting spirit which aroused the ire of even his long-suffering wife. As for his dogs, provided they could run and fight, he cared no more for their looks than for his own; he preferred the animal to be half greyhound, but the other half could be fox-hound, collie, or setter, it mattered nothing to him. They were a wicked, hard-biting crew for all that, and Mr. Cowley, in his flapping linen duster, was a first-class hunter and a good rider. He went almost mad with excitement in every chase. His pack usually hunted coyote, fox, jack-rabbit, and deer; and I have had more than one good run with it.

My own experience is too limited to allow me to pass judgment with certainty as to the relative speed of the different beasts of the chase, especially as there is so much individual variation. I consider the antelope the fleetest of all, however; and in this opinion I am sustained by Colonel Roger D. Williams, of Lexington, Kentucky, who, more than any other American, is entitled to speak upon coursing, and especially upon coursing large game. Colonel Williams, like a true son of Kentucky, has bred his own thoroughbred horses and thoroughbred hounds for many years; and during a series of long hunting trips extending over nearly a quarter of a century he has tried his pack on almost every game animal to be found among the foothills of the Rockies and on the great plains. His dogs, both smooth-haired greyhounds and rough-coated deer-hounds, have been bred by him for generations with a special view to the chase of big game—not merely of hares; they are large animals, excelling not only in speed but in strength, endurance, and ferocious courage. The survivors of his old pack are literally seamed all over with the scars of innumerable battles. When several dogs were together they would stop a bull elk, and fearlessly assail a bear or cougar. This pack scored many a triumph over blacktail, whitetail, and prong-buck. For a few hundred yards the deer were very fast; but in a run of any duration the antelope showed much greater speed, and gave the dogs far more trouble, although always overtaken in the end, if a good start had been obtained. Colonel Williams is a firm believer in the power of the thoroughbred horse to outrun any animal that breathes, in a long chase; he has not infrequently run down deer, when they were jumped some miles from cover; and on two or three occasions he ran down uninjured antelope, but in each case only after a desperate ride of miles, which in one instance resulted in the death of his gallant horse.

This coursing on the prairie, especially after big game, is an exceedingly manly and attractive sport; the furious galloping, often over rough ground with an occasional deep washout or gully, the sight of the gallant hounds running and tackling, and the exhilaration of the pure air and wild surrounding, all combine to give it a peculiar zest. But there is really less need of bold and skilful horsemanship than in the otherwise less attractive and more artificial sport of foxhunting, or riding to hounds, in a closed and long-settled country.

Those of us who are in part of Southern blood have a hereditary right to be fond of cross-country riding; for our forefathers in Virginia, Georgia, or the Carolinas, have for six generations followed the fox with horse, horn, and hound. In the long-settled northern states the sport has been less popular, though much more so now than formerly; yet it has always existed, here and there, and in certain places has been followed quite steadily.

In no place in the Northeast is hunting the wild red fox put on a more genuine and healthy basis than in the Genesee Valley, in central New York. There has always been fox-hunting in this valley, the farmers having good horses and being fond of sport; but it was conducted in a very irregular, primitive manner, until some twenty years ago Mr. Austin Wadsworth turned his attention to it. He has been master of fox-hounds ever since, and no pack in the country has yielded better sport than his, or has brought out harder riders among the men and stronger jumpers among the horses. Mr. Wadsworth began his hunting by picking up some of the various trencher-fed hounds of the neighborhood, the hunting of that period being managed on the principle of each farmer bringing to the meet the hound or hounds he happened to possess, and appearing on foot or horseback as his fancy dictated. Having gotten together some of these native hounds and started fox-hunting in localities where the ground was so open as to necessitate following the chase on horseback, Mr. Wadsworth imported a number of dogs from the best English kennels. He found these to be much faster than the American dogs and more accustomed to work together, but less enduring, and without such good noses. The American hounds were very obstinate and self-willed. Each wished to work out the trail for himself. But once found, they would puzzle it out, no matter how cold, and would follow it if necessary for a day and night. By a judicious crossing of the two Mr. Wadsworth finally got his present fine pack, which for its own particular work on its own ground would be hard to beat. The country ridden over is well wooded, and there are many foxes. The abundance of cover, however, naturally decreases the number of kills. It is a very fertile land, and there are few farming regions more beautiful, for it is prevented from being too tame in aspect by the number of bold hills and deep ravines. Most of the fences are high posts-and-rails or "snake" fences, although there is an occasional stone wall, haha, or water-jump. The steepness of the ravines and the density of the timber make it necessary for a horse to be sure-footed and able to scramble anywhere, and the fences are so high that none but very good jumpers can possibly follow the pack. Most of the horses used are bred by the farmers in the neighborhood, or are from Canada, and they usually have thoroughbred or trotting-stock blood in them.

One of the pleasantest days I ever passed in the saddle was after Mr. Wadsworth's hounds. I was staying with him at the time, in company with my friend Senator Cabot Lodge, of Boston. The meet was about twelve miles distant from the house. It was only a small field of some twenty-five riders, but there was not one who did not mean going. I was mounted on a young horse, a powerful, big-boned black, a great jumper, though perhaps a trifle hot-headed. Lodge was on a fine bay, which could both run and jump. There were two or three other New Yorkers and Bostonians present, several men who had come up from Buffalo for the run, a couple of retired army officers, a number of farmers from the neighborhood; and finally several members of a noted local family of hard riders, who formed a class by themselves, all having taken naturally to every variety of horsemanship from earliest infancy.

It was a thoroughly democratic assemblage; every one was there for sport, and nobody cared an ounce how he or anybody else was dressed. Slouch hats, brown coats, corduroy breeches, and leggings, or boots, were the order of the day. We cast off in a thick wood. The dogs struck a trail almost immediately and were off with clamorous yelping, while the hunt thundered after them like a herd of buffaloes. We went headlong down the hillside into and across a brook. Here the trail led straight up a sheer bank. Most of the riders struck off to the left for an easier place, which was unfortunate for them, for the eight of us who went straight up the side (one man's horse falling back with him) were the only ones who kept on terms with the hounds. Almost as soon as we got to the top of the bank we came out of the woods over a low but awkward rail fence, where one of our number, who was riding a very excitable sorrel colt, got a fall. This left but six, including the whip. There were two or three large fields with low fences; then we came to two high, stiff doubles, the first real jumping of the day, the fences being over four feet six, and so close together that the horses barely had a chance to gather themselves. We got over, however, crossed two or three stump-strewn fields, galloped through an open wood, picked our way across a marshy spot, jumped a small brook and two or three stiff fences, and then came a check. Soon the hounds recovered the line and swung off to the right, back across four or five fields, so as to enable the rest of the hunt, by making an angle, to come up. Then we jumped over a very high board fence into the main road, out of it again, and on over plowed fields and grass lands, separated by stiff snake fences. The run had been fast and the horses were beginning to tail. By the time we suddenly rattled down into a deep ravine and scrambled up the other side through thick timber there were but four of us left, Lodge and myself being two of the lucky ones. Beyond this ravine we came to one of the worst jumps of the day, a fence out of the wood, which was practicable only at one spot, where a kind of cattle trail led up to a panel. It was within an inch or two of five feet high. However, the horses, thoroughly trained to timber jumping and to rough and hard scrambling in awkward places, and by this time well quieted, took the bars without mistake, each one in turn trotting or cantering up to within a few yards, then making a couple of springs and bucking over with a great twist of the powerful haunches. I may explain that there was not a horse of the four that had not a record of five feet six inches in the ring. We now got into a perfect tangle of ravines, and the fox went to earth; and though we started one or two more in the course of the afternoon, we did not get another really first-class run.

At Geneseo the conditions for the enjoyment of this sport are exceptionally favorable. In the Northeast generally, although there are now a number of well-established hunts, at least nine out of ten runs are after a drag. Most of the hunts are in the neighborhood of great cities, and are mainly kept up by young men who come from them. A few of these are men of leisure, who can afford to devote their whole time to pleasure; but much the larger number are men in business, who work hard and are obliged to make their sports accommodate themselves to their more serious occupations. Once or twice a week they can get off for an after noon's ride across country, and they then wish to be absolutely certain of having their run, and of having it at the appointed time; and the only way to ensure this is to have a drag-hunt. It is not the lack of foxes that has made the sport so commonly take the form of riding to drag-hounds, but rather the fact that the majority of those who keep it up are hard-working business men who wish to make the most out of every moment of the little time they can spare from their regular occupations. A single ride across country, or an afternoon at polo, will yield more exercise, fun, and excitement than can be got out of a week's decorous and dull riding in the park, and many young fellows have waked up to this fact.

At one time I did a good deal of hunting with the Meadowbrook hounds, in the northern part of Long Island. There were plenty of foxes around us, both red and gray, but partly for the reasons given above, and partly because the covers were so large and so nearly continuous, they were not often hunted, although an effort was always made to have one run every week or so after a wild fox, in order to give a chance for the hounds to be properly worked and to prevent the runs from becoming a mere succession of steeplechases. The sport was mainly drag-hunting, and was most exciting, as the fences were high and the pace fast. The Long Island country needs a peculiar style of horse, the first requisite being that he shall be a very good and high timber jumper. Quite a number of crack English and Irish hunters have at different times been imported, and some of them have turned out pretty well; but when they first come over they are utterly unable to cross our country, blundering badly at the high timber. Few of them have done as well as the American horses. I have hunted half a dozen times in England, with the Pytchely, Essex, and North Warwickshire, and it seems to me probable that English thoroughbreds, in a grass country, and over the peculiar kinds of obstacles they have on the other side of the water, would gallop away from a field of our Long Island horses; for they have speed and bottom, and are great weight carriers. But on our own ground, where the cross-country riding is more like leaping a succession of five and six-bar gates than anything else, they do not as a rule, in spite of the enormous prices paid for them, show themselves equal to the native stock. The highest recorded jump, seven feet two inches, was made by the American horse Filemaker, which I saw ridden in the very front by Mr. H. L. Herbert, in the hunt at Sagamore Hill, about to be described.

When I was a member of the Meadowbrook hunt, most of the meets were held within a dozen miles or so of the kennels: at Farmingdale, Woodbury, Wheatly, Locust Valley, Syosset, or near any one of twenty other queer, quaint old Long Island hamlets. They were almost always held in the afternoon, the business men who had come down from the city jogging over behind the hounds to the appointed place, where they were met by the men who had ridden over direct from their country-houses. If the meet was an important one, there might be a crowd of onlookers in every kind of trap, from a four-in-hand drag to a spider-wheeled buggy drawn by a pair of long-tailed trotters, the money value of which many times surpassed that of the two best hunters in the whole field. Now and then a breakfast would be given the hunt at some country-house, when the whole day was devoted to the sport; perhaps after wild foxes in the morning, with a drag in the afternoon.

After one meet, at Sagamore Hill, I had the curiosity to go on foot over the course we had taken, measuring the jumps; for it is very difficult to form a good estimate of a fence's height when in the field, and five feet of timber seems a much easier thing to take when sitting around the fire after dinner than it does when actually faced while the hounds are running. On the particular hunt in question we ran about ten miles, at a rattling pace, with only two checks, crossing somewhat more than sixty fences, most of them post-and-rails, stiff as steel, the others being of the kind called "Virginia" or snake, and not more than ten or a dozen in the whole lot under four feet in height. The highest measured five feet and half an inch, two others were four feet eleven, and nearly a third of the number averaged about four and a half. There were also several rather awkward doubles. When the hounds were cast off some forty riders were present, but the first fence was a savage one, and stopped all who did not mean genuine hard going. Twenty-six horses crossed it, one of them ridden by a lady. A mile or so further on, before there had been a chance for much tailing, we came to a five-bar gate, out of a road—a jump of just four feet five inches from the take-off. Up to this, of course, we went one at a time, at a trot or hand-gallop, and twenty-five horses cleared it in succession without a single refusal and with but one mistake.

Owing to the severity of the pace, combined with the average height of the timber (although no one fence was of phenomenally noteworthy proportions), a good many falls took place, resulting in an unusually large percentage of accidents. The master partly dislocated one knee, another man broke two ribs, and another—the present writer—broke his arm. However, almost all of us managed to struggle through to the end in time to see the death.

On this occasion I owed my broken arm to the fact that my horse, a solemn animal originally taken out of a buggy, though a very clever fencer, was too coarse to gallop alongside the blooded beasts against which he was pitted. But he was so easy in his gaits, and so quiet, being ridden with only a snaffle, that there was no difficulty in following to the end of the run. I had divers adventures on this horse. Once I tried a pair of so-called "safety" stirrups, which speedily fell out, and I had to ride through the run without any, at the cost of several tumbles. Much the best hunter I ever owned was a sorrel horse named Sagamore. He was from Geneseo, was fast, a remarkably good jumper, of great endurance, as quick on his feet as a cat, and with a dauntless heart. He never gave me a fall, and generally enabled me to see all the run.

It would be very unfair to think the sport especially dangerous on account of the occasional accidents that happen. A man who is fond of riding, but who sets a good deal of value, either for the sake of himself, his family, or his business, upon his neck and limbs, can hunt with much safety if he gets a quiet horse, a safe fencer, and does not try to stay in the front rank. Most accidents occur to men on green or wild horses, or else to those who keep in front only at the expense of pumping their mounts; and a fall with a done-out beast is always peculiarly disagreeable. Most falls, however, do no harm whatever to either horse or rider, and after they have picked themselves up and shaken themselves, the couple ought to be able to go on just as well as ever. Of course a man who wishes to keep in the first flight must expect to face a certain number of tumbles; but even he will probably not be hurt at all, and he can avoid many a mishap by easing up his horse whenever he can—

that is, by always taking a gap when possible, going at the lowest panel of every fence, and not calling on his animal for all there is in him unless it can not possibly be avoided. It must be remembered that hard riding is a very different thing from good riding; though a good rider to hounds must also at times ride hard.

Cross-country riding in the rough is not a difficult thing to learn; always provided the would-be learner is gifted with or has acquired a fairly stout heart, for a constitutionally timid person is out of place in the hunting field. A really finished cross-country rider, a man who combines hand and seat, heart and head, is of course rare; the standard is too high for most of us to hope to reach. But it is comparatively easy to acquire a light hand and a capacity to sit fairly well down in the saddle; and when a man has once got these, he will find no especial difficulty in following the hounds on a trained hunter.

Fox-hunting is a great sport, but it is as foolish to make a fetish of it as it is to decry it. The fox is hunted merely because there is no larger game to follow. As long as wolves, deer, or antelope remain in the land, and in a country where hounds and horsemen can work, no one would think of following the fox. It is pursued because the bigger beasts of the chase have been killed out. In England it has reached its present prominence only within two centuries; nobody followed the fox while the stag and the boar were common. At the present day, on Exmoor, where the wild stag is still found, its chase ranks ahead of that of the fox. It is not really the hunting proper which is the point in fox-hunting. It is the horsemanship, the galloping and jumping, and the being out in the open air. Very naturally, however, men who have passed their lives as fox-hunters grow to regard the chase and the object of it alike with superstitious veneration. They attribute almost mythical characters to the animal. I know some of my good Virginian friends, for instance, who seriously believe that the Virginia red fox is a beast quite unparalleled for speed and endurance no less than for cunning. This is of course a mistake. Compared with a wolf, an antelope, or even a deer, the fox's speed and endurance do not stand very high. A good pack of hounds starting him close would speedily run into him in the open. The reason that the hunts last so long in some cases is because of the nature of the ground which favors the fox at the expense of the dogs, because of his having the advantage in the start, and because of his cunning in turning to account everything which will tell in his favor and against his pursuers. In the same way I know plenty of English friends who speak with bated breath of fox-hunting but look down upon riding to drag-hounds. Of course there is a difference in the two sports, and the fun of actually hunting the wild beast in the one case more than compensates for the fact that in the other the riding is apt to be harder and the jumping higher; but both sports are really artificial, and in their essentials alike. To any man who has hunted big game in a wild country the stress laid on the differences between them seems a little absurd, in fact cockney. It is of course nothing against either that it is artificial; so are all sports in long-civilized countries, from lacrosse to ice yachting.

It is amusing to see how natural it is for each man to glorify the sport to which he has been accustomed at the expense of any other. The old-school French sportsman, for instance, who followed the boar, stag, and hare with his hounds, always looked down upon the chase of the fox; whereas the average Englishman not only asserts but seriously believes that no other kind of chase can compare with it, although in actual fact the very points in which the Englishman is superior to the Continental sportsman — that is, in hard and straight riding and jumping — are those which drag-hunting tends to develop rather more than fox-hunting proper. In the mere hunting itself the Continental sportsman is often unsurpassed.

Once beyond the Missouri, I met an expatriated German baron, an unfortunate who had failed utterly in the rough life of the frontier. He was living in a squalid little hut, almost unfurnished, but studded around with the diminutive horns of the European roebuck. These were the only treasures he had taken with him to remind him of his former life, and he was never tired of describing what fun it was to shoot roebucks when driven by the little crooked-legged *dachshunds*. There were plenty of deer and antelope round about, yielding good sport to any rifleman, but this exile cared nothing for them; they were not roebucks, and they could not be chased with his beloved *dachshunds*. So, among my neighbors in the cattle country, is a gentleman from France, a very successful ranchman, and a thoroughly good fellow; he cares nothing for hunting big game, and will not go after it, but is devoted to shooting cotton-tails in the snow, this being a pastime having much resemblance to one of the recognized sports of his own land.

However, our own people afford precisely similar instances. I have met plenty of men accustomed to killing wild turkeys and deer with small-bore rifles in the southern forests who, when they got on the plains and in the Rockies, were absolutely helpless. They not only failed to become proficient in the art of killing big game at long ranges with the large-bore rifle, at the cost of fatiguing tramps, but they had a positive distaste for the sport and would never allow that it equaled their own stealthy hunts in Southern forests. So I know plenty of men, experts with the shotgun, who honestly prefer shooting quail in the East over well-trained setters or pointers, to the hardier, manlier sports of the wilderness.

As it is with hunting, so it is with riding. The cowboy's scorn of every method of riding save his own is as profound and as ignorant as is that of the school rider, jockey, or fox-hunter. The truth is that each of these is best in his own sphere and is at a disadvantage when made to do the work of any of the others. For all-around riding and horsemanship, I think the West Point graduate is somewhat ahead of any of them. Taken as a class, however, and compared with other classes as numerous, and not with a few exceptional individuals, the cowboy, like the Rocky Mountain stage-driver, has no superiors anywhere for his own work; and they are fine fellows, these iron-nerved reinsmen and rough-riders.

When Buffalo Bill took his cowboys to Europe they made a practice in England, France, Germany, and Italy of offering to break and ride, in their own fashion, any horse given them. They were frequently given spoiled animals from the cavalry services in the different countries through which they passed, animals with which the trained horse-breakers of the European armies could do nothing; and yet in almost all cases the cowpunchers and bronco-busters with Buffalo Bill mastered these beasts as readily as they did their own Western horses. At their own work of mastering and riding rough horses they could not be matched by their more civilized rivals; but I have great doubts whether they in turn would not have been beaten if they had essayed kinds of horsemanship utterly alien to their past experience, such as riding mettled thoroughbreds in a steeple-chase, or the like. Other things being equal (which, however, they generally are not), a bad, big horse fed on oats offers a rather more difficult problem than a bad little horse fed on grass. After Buffalo Bill's men had returned, I occasionally heard it said that they had tried cross-country riding in England, and had shown themselves pre-eminently skilful thereat, doing better than the English fox-hunters, but this I take the liberty to disbelieve. I was in England at the time, hunted occasionally myself, and was with many of the men who were all the time riding in the most famous hunts; men, too, who were greatly impressed with the exhibitions of rough riding then being given by Buffalo Bill and his men, and who talked of them much; and yet I never, at the time, heard of an instance in which one of the cowboys rode to hounds with any marked success.[1] In the same way I have sometimes in New York or London heard of men who, it was alleged, had been out West and proved better riders than the bronco-busters themselves, just as I have heard of similar men who were able to go out hunting in the Rockies or on the plains and get more game than the Western hunters; but in the course of a long experience in the West I have yet to see any of these men, whether from the eastern states or from Europe, actually show such superiority or perform such feats.

It would be interesting to compare the performances of the Australian stock-riders with those of our own cowpunchers, both in cow-work and in riding. The Australians have an entirely different kind of saddle, and the use of the rope is unknown among them. A couple of years ago the famous Western rifle-shot, Carver, took some cowboys out to Australia, and I am informed that many of the Australians began themselves to practice with the rope after seeing the way it was used by the Americans. An Australian gentleman, Mr. A. J. Sage, of Melbourne, to whom I had written asking how the saddles and styles of riding compared, answered me as follows:

"With regard to saddles, here it is a moot question which is the better, yours or ours, for buck-jumpers. Carver's boys rode in their own saddles against our Victorians in theirs, all on Australian buckers, and honors seemed easy. Each was good in his own style, but the horses were not what I should call really good buckers, such as you might get on a back station, and so there was nothing in the show that could unseat the cowboys. It is only back in the bush that you can get a really good bucker. I have often seen one of them put both man and saddle off."

This last is a feat I have myself seen performed in the West. I suppose the amount of it is that both the American and the Australian rough riders are, for their own work, just as good as men possibly can be.

One spring I had to leave the East in the midst of the hunting season, to join a round-up in the cattle country of western Dakota, and it was curious to compare the totally different styles of riding of the cowboys and the cross-country men. A stock-saddle weighs thirty or forty pounds instead of ten or fifteen and needs an utterly different seat from that adopted in the East. A cowboy rides with very long stirrups, sitting forked well down between his high pommel and cantle, and depends upon balance as well as on the grip of his thighs. In cutting out a steer from a herd, in breaking a vicious wild horse, in sitting a bucking bronco, in stopping a night stampede of many hundred maddened animals, or in the performance of a hundred other feats of reckless and daring horsemanship, the cowboy is absolutely unequaled; and when he has his own horse gear he sits his animal with the ease of a centaur. Yet he is quite helpless the first time he gets astride one of the small Eastern saddles. One summer, while purchasing cattle in Iowa, one of my ranch foremen had to get on an ordinary saddle to ride out of town and see a bunch of steers. He is perhaps the best rider on the ranch, and will without hesitation mount and master beasts that I doubt if the boldest rider in one of our Eastern hunts would care to tackle; yet his uneasiness on the new saddle was fairly comical. At first he did not dare to trot, and the least plunge of the horse bid fair to unseat him, nor did he begin to get accustomed to the situation until the very end of the journey. In fact, the two kinds of riding are so very different that a man only accustomed to one feels almost as ill at ease when he first tries the other as if he had never sat on a horse's back before. It is rather funny to see a man who only knows one kind, and is conceited enough to think that that is really the only kind worth knowing, when first he is brought into contact with the other. Two or three times I have known men try to follow hounds on stock-saddles, which are about as ill-suited for the purpose as they well can be; while it is even more laughable to see some young fellow from the East or from England, who thinks he knows entirely too much about horses to be taught by barbarians, attempt in his turn to do cow-work with his ordinary riding or hunting rig. It must be said, however, that in all probability cowboys would learn to ride well across country much sooner than the average cross-country rider would master the dashing and peculiar style of horsemanship shown by those whose life business is to guard the wandering herds of the great Western plains.

Of course, riding to hounds, like all sports in long settled, thickly peopled countries, fails to develop in its followers some of the hardy qualities necessarily incident to the wilder pursuits of the mountain and the forest. While I was on the frontier I was struck by the fact that of the men from the eastern states or from England who had shown themselves at home to be good riders to hounds or had made their records as college athletes, a larger proportion failed in the life of the wilderness than was the case among those who had gained their experience in such rough pastimes as mountaineering in the high Alps, winter caribou-hunting in Canada, or deer-stalking—not deer-driving—in Scotland.

Nevertheless, of all sports possible in civilized countries, riding to hounds is perhaps the best if followed as it should be, for the sake of the strong excitement, with as much simplicity as possible, and not merely as a fashionable amusement. It tends to develop moral no less than physical qualities; the rider needs nerve and head; he must possess daring and resolution, as well as a good deal of bodily skill and a certain amount of wiry toughness and endurance.

CHAPTER VIII

WOLVES AND WOLF-HOUNDS

THE wolf is the archetype of ravin, the beast of waste and desolation. It is still found scattered thinly throughout all the wilder portions of the United States, but has everywhere retreated from the advance of civilization.

Wolves show an infinite variety in color, size, physical formation, and temper. Almost all the varieties intergrade with one another, however, so that it is very difficult to draw a hard and fast line between any two of them. Nevertheless, west of the Mississippi there are found two distinct types. One is the wolf proper, or big wolf, specifically akin to the wolves of the eastern states. The other is the little coyote, or prairie wolf. The coyote and the big wolf are found together in almost all the wilder districts from the Rio Grande to the valleys of the Upper Missouri and the Upper Columbia. Throughout this region there is always a sharp line of demarcation, especially in size, between the coyotes and the big wolves of any given district; but in certain districts the big wolves are very much larger than their brethren in other districts. In the upper Columbia country, for instance, they are very large; along the Rio Grande they are small. Dr. Hart Merriam informs me that, according to his experience, the coyote is largest in Southern California. In many respects the coyote differs altogether in habits from its big relative. For one thing it is far more tolerant of man. In some localities coyotes are more numerous around settlements, and even in the close vicinity of large towns, than they are in the frowning and desolate fastnesses haunted by their grim elder brother.

Big wolves vary far more in color than the coyotes do. I have seen white, black, red, yellow, brown, gray, and grizzled skins, and others representing every shade between, although usually each locality has its prevailing tint. The grizzled, gray, and brown often have precisely the coat of the coyote. The difference in size among wolves of different localities, and even of the same locality, is quite remarkable, and so, curiously enough, is the difference in the size of the teeth, in some cases even when the body of one wolf is as big as that of another. I have seen wolves from Texas and New Mexico which were undersized, slim animals with rather small tusks, in no way to be compared to the long-toothed giants of their race that dwell in the heavily timbered mountains of the Northwest and in the far North. As a rule, the teeth of the coyote are relatively smaller than those of the gray wolf.

Formerly wolves were incredibly abundant in certain parts of the country, notably on the great plains, where they were known as buffalo wolves, and were regular attendants on the great herds of the bison. Every traveler and hunter of the old days knew them as among the most common sights of the plains, and they followed the hunting parties and emigrant trains for the sake of the scraps left in camp. Now, however, there is no district in which they are really abundant. The wolfers, or professional wolf-hunters, who killed them by poisoning for the sake of their fur, and the cattle men, who likewise killed them by poisoning because of their raids on the herds, have doubtless been the chief instruments in working their decimation on the plains. In the '70s, and even in the early '80s, many tens of thousands of wolves were killed by the wolfers in Montana and northern Wyoming and western Dakota. Nowadays the surviving wolves of the plains have learned caution; they no longer move abroad at midday, and still less do they dream of hanging on the footsteps of hunter and traveler. Instead of being one of the most common they have become one of the rarest sights of the plains. A hunter may wander far and wide through the plains for months nowadays and never see a wolf, though he will probably see many coyotes. However, the diminution goes on, not steadily but by fits and starts, and, moreover, the beasts now and then change their abodes, and appear in numbers in places where they have been scarce for a long period. In the present winter of 1892-'93 big wolves are more plentiful in the neighborhood of my ranch than they have been for ten years, and have worked some havoc among the cattle and young horses. The cowboys have been carrying on the usual vindictive campaign against them; a number have been poisoned, and a number of others have fallen victims to their greediness, the cowboys surprising them when gorged to repletion on the carcass of a colt or calf, and, in consequence, unable to run, so that they are easily ridden down, roped, and then dragged to death.

Yet even the slaughter wrought by man in certain localities does not seem adequate to explain the scarcity or extinction of wolves, throughout the country at large. In most places they are not followed any more eagerly than are the other large beasts of prey, and they are usually followed with less success. Of all animals the wolf is the shyest and hardest to slay. It is almost or quite as difficult to still-hunt as the cougar, and is far more difficult to kill with hounds, traps, or poison; yet it scarcely holds its own as well as the great cat, and it does not begin to hold its own as well as the bear, a beast certainly more readily killed, and one which produces fewer young at a birth. Throughout the East the black bear is common in many localities from which the wolf has vanished completely. It at present exists in very scanty numbers in northern Maine and the Adirondacks; is almost or quite extinct in Pennsylvania; lingers here and there in the mountains from West Virginia to East Tennessee, and is found in Florida; but is everywhere less abundant than the bear. It is possible that this destruction of the wolves is due to some disease among them, perhaps to hydrophobia, a terrible malady from which it is known that they suffer greatly at times. Perhaps the bear is helped by its habit of hibernating, which frees it from most dangers during winter; but this cannot be the complete explanation, for in the South it does not hibernate, and yet holds its own as well as in the North. What makes it all the more curious that the American wolf should disappear sooner than the bear is that the reverse is the case with the allied species of Europe, where the bear is much sooner killed out of the land.

Indeed the differences of this sort between nearly related animals are literally inexplicable. Much of the difference in temperament between such closely allied species as the American and European bears and wolves is doubtless due to their surroundings and to the instincts they have inherited through many generations; but for much of the variation it is not possible to offer any explanation. In the same way there are certain physical differences for which it is very hard to account, as the same conditions seem to operate in directly reverse ways with different animals. No one can explain the process of natural selection which has resulted in the otter of America being larger than the otter of Europe, while the badger is smaller; in the mink being with us a much stouter animal than its Scandinavian and Russian kinsman, while the reverse is true of our sable or pine marten. No one can say why the European red deer should be a pigmy compared to its giant brother, the American wapiti; why the Old World elk should average smaller in size than the almost indistinguishable New World moose; and yet the bison of Lithuania and the Caucasus be on the whole larger and more formidable than its American cousin. In the same way no one can tell why under like conditions some game, such as the white goat and the spruce grouse, should be tamer than other closely allied species, like the mountain sheep and ruffed grouse. No one can say why on the whole the wolf of Scandinavia and northern Russia should be larger and more dangerous than the average wolf of the Rocky Mountains, while between the bears of the same regions the comparison must be exactly reversed.

The difference even among the wolves of different sections of our own country is very notable. It may be true that the species as a whole is rather weak and less ferocious than the European wolf;

but it is certainly not true of the wolves of certain localities. The great timber wolf of the central and northern chains of the Rockies and coast ranges is in every way a more formidable creature than the buffalo wolf of the plains, although they intergrade. The skins and skulls of the wolves of northwestern Montana and Washington which I have seen were quite as large and showed quite as stout claws and teeth as the skins and skulls of Russian and Scandinavian wolves, and I believe that these great timber wolves are in every way as formidable as their Old World kinsfolk. However, they live where they come in contact with a population of rifle-bearing frontier hunters, who are very different from European peasants or Asiatic tribesmen; and they have, even when most hungry, a wholesome dread of human beings. Yet I doubt if an unarmed man would be entirely safe should he, while alone in the forest in mid-winter, encounter a fair-sized pack of ravenously hungry timber wolves.

A full-grown dog-wolf of the northern Rockies, in exceptional instances, reaches a height of thirty-two inches and a weight of 130 pounds; a big buffalo wolf of the upper Missouri stands thirty or thirty-one inches at the shoulder and weighs about 110 pounds. A Texan wolf may not reach over eighty pounds. The bitch-wolves are smaller; and moreover there is often great variation even in the wolves of closely neighboring localities.

The wolves of the Southern plains were not often formidable to large animals, even in the days when they most abounded. They rarely attacked the horses of the hunter, and indeed were but little regarded by these experienced animals. They were much more likely to gnaw off the lariat with which the horse was tied, than to try to molest the steed himself. They preferred to prey on young animals, or on the weak and disabled. They rarely molested a full-grown cow or steer, still less a full-grown buffalo, and, if they did attack such an animal, it was only when emboldened by numbers. In the plains of the upper Missouri and Saskatchewan the wolf was, and is, more dangerous, while in the northern Rockies his courage and ferocity attain their highest pitch. Near my own ranch the wolves have sometimes committed great depredations on cattle, but they seem to have queer freaks of slaughter. Usually they prey only upon calves and sickly animals; but in midwinter I have known one single-handed to attack and kill a well-grown steer or cow, disabling its quarry by rapid snaps at the hams or flanks. Only rarely have I known it to seize by the throat. Colts are likewise a favorite prey, but with us wolves rarely attack full-grown horses. They are sometimes very bold in their assaults, falling on the stock while immediately around the ranch houses. They even venture into the hamlet of Medora itself at night—as the coyotes sometimes do by day. In the spring of '92 we put on some Eastern two-year-old steers; they arrived, and were turned loose from the stockyards, in a snowstorm, though it was in early May. Next morning we found that one had been seized, slain, and partially devoured by a big wolf at the very gate of the stockyard; probably the beast had seen it standing near the yard after nightfall, feeling miserable after its journey, in the storm and its unaccustomed surroundings, and had been emboldened to make the assault so near town by the evident helplessness of the prey.

The big timber wolves of the northern Rocky Mountains attack every four-footed beast to be found where they live. They are far from contenting themselves with hunting deer and snapping up the pigs and sheep of the farm. When the weather gets cold and food scarce they band together in small parties, perhaps of four or five individuals, and then assail anything, even a bear or a panther. A bull elk or bull moose, when on its guard, makes a most dangerous fight; but a single wolf will frequently master the cow of either animal, as well as domestic cattle and horses. In attacking such large game, however, the wolves like to act in concert, one springing at the animal's head, and attracting its attention, while the other hamstrings it. Nevertheless, one such big wolf will kill an ordinary horse. A man I knew, who was engaged in packing into the Cœur d'Alenes, once witnessed such a feat on the part of a wolf. He was taking his pack train down into a valley when he saw a horse grazing therein; it had been turned loose by another packing outfit, because it became exhausted. He lost sight of it as the trail went down a zigzag, and while it was thus out of sight he suddenly heard it utter the appalling scream, unlike and more dreadful than any other sound, which a horse only utters in extreme fright or agony. The scream was repeated, and as he came in sight again he saw that a great wolf had attacked the horse. The poor animal had been bitten terribly in its haunches and was cowering upon them, while the wolf stood and looked at it a few paces off. In a moment or two the horse partially recovered and made a desperate bound forward, starting at full gallop. Immediately the wolf was after it, overhauled it in three or four jumps, and then seized it by the hock, while its legs were extended, with such violence as to bring it completely back on its haunches. It again screamed piteously; and this time with a few savage snaps the wolf hamstrung and partially disemboweled it, and it fell over, having made no attempt to defend itself. I have heard of more than one incident of this kind. If a horse is a good fighter, however, as occasionally, though not often, happens, it is a most difficult prey for any wild beast, and some veteran horses have no fear of wolves whatsoever, well knowing that they can either strike them down with their forefeet or repulse them by lashing out behind.

Wolves are cunning beasts and will often try to lull their prey into unsuspicion by playing round and cutting capers. I once saw a young deer and a wolf-cub together near the hut of the settler who had captured both. The wolf was just old enough to begin to feel vicious and bloodthirsty, and to show symptoms of attacking the deer. On the occasion in question he got loose and ran toward it, but it turned, and began to hit him with its forefeet, seemingly in sport; whereat he rolled over on his back before it, and acted like a puppy at play. Soon it turned and walked off; immediately the wolf, with bristling hair, crawled after, and with a pounce seized it by the haunch, and would doubtless have murdered the bleating, struggling creature, had not the bystanders interfered.

Where there are no domestic animals, wolves feed on almost anything from a mouse to an elk. They are redoubted enemies of foxes. They are easily able to overtake them in fair chase, and kill numbers. If the fox can get into the underbrush, however, he can dodge around much faster than the wolf, and so escape pursuit. Sometimes one wolf will try to put a fox out of a cover while another waits outside to snap him up. Moreover, the wolf kills even closer kinsfolk than the fox. When pressed by hunger it will undoubtedly sometimes seize a coyote, tear it in pieces and devour it, although during most of the year the two animals live in perfect harmony. I once myself, while out in the deep snow, came across the remains of a coyote that had been killed in this manner. Wolves are also very fond of the flesh of dogs, and if they get a chance promptly kill and eat any dog they can master—and there are but few that they cannot. Nevertheless, I have been told of one instance in which a wolf struck up an extraordinary friendship with a strayed dog, and the two lived and hunted together for many months, being frequently seen by the settlers of the locality. This occurred near Thompson's Falls, Montana.

Usually wolves are found singly, in pairs, or in family parties, each having a large beat over which it regularly hunts, and also at times shifting its ground and traveling immense distances in order to take up a temporary abode in some new locality—for they are great wanderers. It is only under stress of severe weather that they band together in packs. They prefer to creep on their prey and seize it by a sudden pounce, but, unlike the cougar, they also run it down in fair chase. Their slouching, tireless gallop enables them often to overtake deer, antelope, or other quarry; though under favorable circumstances, especially if near a lake, the latter frequently escape. Whether wolves run cunning I do not know; but I think they must, for coyotes certainly do. A coyote cannot run down a jack-rabbit; but two or three working together will often catch one. Once I saw three start a jack, which ran right away from them; but they spread out, and followed. Pretty soon the jack turned slightly, and ran near one of the outside ones, saw it, became much frightened, and turned at right angles, so as soon to nearly run into the other outside one, which had kept straight on. This happened several times, and then the confused jack lay down under a sage-bush and was seized. So I have seen two coyotes attempting to get at a newly dropped antelope kid. One would make a feint of attack, and lure the dam into a rush at him, while the other stole round to get at the kid. The dam, as always with these spirited little prong-bucks, made a good fight, and kept the assailants at bay; yet I think they would have succeeded in the end, had I not interfered. Coyotes are bold and cunning in raiding the settlers' barnyards for lambs and hens; and they have an especial liking for tame cats. If there are coyotes in the neighborhood a cat which gets into the habit of wandering from home is surely lost.

Though I have never known wolves to attack a man, yet in the wilder portion of the far Northwest I have heard them come around camp very close, growling so savagely as to make one almost reluctant to leave the camp fire and go out into the darkness unarmed. Once I was camped in the fall near a lonely little lake in the mountains, by the edge of quite a broad stream. Soon after nightfall three or four wolves came around camp and kept me awake by their sinister and dismal howling. Two or three times they came so close to the fire that I could hear them snap their jaws and growl, and at one time I positively thought that they intended to try to get into camp, so excited were they by the smell of the fresh meat. After a while they stopped howling; and then all was silent for an hour or so. I let the fire go out and was turning into bed when I suddenly heard some animal of considerable size come down to the stream nearly opposite me and begin to splash across, first wading, then swimming. It was pitch dark and I could not possibly see, but I felt sure it was a wolf. However after coming half-way over it changed its mind and swam back to the opposite bank; nor did I see or hear anything more of the night marauders.

Five or six times on the plains or on my ranch I have had shots at wolves, always obtained by accident and always, I regret to say, missed. Often the wolf when seen was running at full speed for cover, or else was so far off that though motionless my shots went wide of it. But once have I with my own rifle killed a wolf, and this was while traveling with a pack train in the mountains. We had been making considerable noise, and I never understood how an animal so wary permitted our near approach. He did, nevertheless, and just as we came to a little stream which we were to ford I saw him get on a dead log some thirty yards distant and walk slowly off with his eyes turned toward us. The first shot smashed his shoulders and brought him down.

The wolf is one of the animals which can only be hunted successfully with dogs. Most dogs however do not take at all kindly to the pursuit. A wolf is a terrible fighter. He will decimate a pack of hounds by rabid snaps with his giant jaws while suffering little damage himself; nor are the ordinary big dogs, supposed to be fighting dogs, able to tackle him without special training. I have known one wolf to kill with a single snap a bulldog which had rushed at it, while another which had entered the yard of a Montana ranch house slew in quick succession both of the large mastiffs by which it was assailed. The immense agility and ferocity of the wild beast, the terrible snap of his long-toothed jaws, and the admirable training in which he always is, give him a great advantage over fat, small-toothed, smooth-skinned dogs, even though they are nominally supposed to belong to the fighting classes. In the way that bench competitions are arranged nowadays this is but natural, as there is no temptation to produce a worthy class of fighting dog when the rewards are given upon technical points wholly unconnected with the dog's usefulness. A prize-winning mastiff or bulldog may be almost useless for the only purposes for which his kind is ever useful at all. A mastiff; if properly trained and of sufficient size, might possibly be able to meet a young or undersized Texan wolf; but I have never seen a dog of this variety which I would esteem a match single-handed for one of the huge timber wolves of western Montana. Even if the dog was the heavier of the two, his teeth and claws would be very much smaller and weaker and his hide less tough. Indeed I have known of but one dog which single-handed encountered and slew a wolf; this was the large vicious mongrel whose feats are recorded in my *Hunting Trips of a Ranchman.*

General Marcy of the United States Army informed me that he once chased a huge wolf which had gotten away with a small trap on its foot. It was, I believe, in Wisconsin, and he had twenty or thirty hounds with him, but they were entirely untrained to wolf-hunting, and proved unable to stop the crippled beast. Few of them would attack it at all, and those that did went at it singly and with a certain hesitation, and so each in turn was disabled by a single terrible snap, and left bleeding on the snow. General Wade Hampton tells me that in the course of his fifty years' hunting with horse and hound in Mississippi, he has on several occasions tried his pack of foxhounds (Southern deer-hounds) after a wolf. He found that it was with the greatest difficulty, however, that he could persuade them to so much as follow the trail. Usually, as soon as they came across it, they would growl, bristle up, and then retreat with their tails between their legs. But one of his dogs ever really tried to master a wolf by itself, and this one paid for its temerity with its life; for while running a wolf in a canebrake the beast turned and tore it to pieces. Finally General Hampton succeeded in getting a number of his hounds so they would at any rate follow the trail in full cry, and thus drive the wolf out of the thicket, and give a chance to the hunter to get a shot. In this way he killed two or three.

The true way to kill wolves, however, is to hunt them with greyhounds on the great plains. Nothing more exciting than this sport can possibly be imagined. It is not always necessary that the greyhounds should be of absolutely pure blood. Prize-winning dogs of high pedigree often prove useless for the purpose. If by careful choice, however, a ranchman can get together a pack composed both of the smooth-haired greyhound and the rough-haired Scotch deer-hound, he can have excellent sport. The greyhounds sometimes do best if they have a slight cross of bulldog in their veins; but this is not necessary. If once a greyhound can be fairly entered to the sport and acquires confidence, then its wonderful agility, its sinewy strength and speed, and the terrible snap with which its jaws come together, render it a most formidable assailant. Nothing can possibly exceed the gallantry with which good greyhounds, when their blood is up, fling themselves on a wolf or any other foe. There does not exist, and there never has existed on the wide earth, a more perfect type of dauntless courage than such a hound. Not Cushing when he steered his little launch through the black night against the great ram *Albemarle*, not Custer dashing into the valley of the Rosebud to die with all his men, not Farragut himself lashed in the rigging of the *Hartford* as she forged past the forts to encounter her ironclad foe, can stand as a more perfect type of dauntless valor.

Once I had the good fortune to witness a very exciting hunt of this character among the foothills of the northern Rockies. I was staying at the house of a friendly cowman, whom I will call Judge Yancy Stump. Judge Yancy Stump was a Democrat who, as he phrased it, had fought for his Democracy; that is, he had been in the Confederate Army. He was at daggers drawn with his nearest neighbor, a cross-grained mountain farmer, who may be known as old man Prindle. Old man Prindle had been in the Union Army, and his Republicanism was of the blackest and most uncompromising type. There was one point, however, on which the two came together. They were exceedingly fond of hunting with hounds. The Judge had three or four track-hounds, and four of what he called swift-hounds, the latter including one pure-bred greyhound bitch of wonderful speed and temper, a dun-colored yelping animal which was a cross between a greyhound and a fox-hound, and two others that were crosses between a greyhound and a wire-haired Scotch deer-hound. Old man Prindle's contribution to the pack consisted of two immense brindled mongrels of great strength and ferocious temper. They were unlike any dogs I have ever seen in this country. Their mother herself was a cross between a bull mastiff and a Newfoundland, while the father was described as being a big dog that belonged to a "Dutch Count." The "Dutch Count" was an outcast German noble, who had drifted to the West, and, after failing in the mines and failing in the cattle country, had died in a squalid log shanty while striving to eke out an existence as a hunter among the foothills. His dog, I presume, from the description given me, must have been a boar-hound or Ulm dog.

As I was very anxious to see a wolf-hunt the Judge volunteered to get one up, and asked old man Prindle to assist, for the sake of his two big fighting dogs; though the very names of the latter, General Grant and Old Abe, were gall and wormwood to the unreconstructed soul of the Judge. Still they were the only dogs anywhere around capable of tackling a savage timber wolf, and without their aid the Judge's own high-spirited animals ran a serious risk of injury, for they were altogether too game to let any beast escape without a struggle.

Luck favored us. Two wolves had killed a calf and dragged it into a long patch of dense brush where there was a little spring, the whole furnishing admirable cover for any wild beast. Early in the morning we started on horseback for this bit of cover, which was some three miles off. The party consisted of the Judge, old man Prindle, a cowboy, myself, and the dogs. The Judge and I carried our rifles and the cowboy his revolver, but old man Prindle had nothing but a heavy whip, for he swore, with many oaths, that no one should interfere with his big dogs, for by themselves they would surely "make the wolf feel sicker than a stuck hog.'" Our shaggy ponies racked along at a five-mile gait over the dewy prairie grass. The two big dogs trotted behind their master, grim and ferocious. The track-hounds were tied in couples, and the beautiful greyhounds loped lightly and gracefully alongside the horses. The country was fine. A mile to our right a small plains river wound in long curves between banks fringed with cottonwoods. Two or three miles to our left the foothills rose sheer and bare, with clumps of black pine and cedar in their gorges. We rode over gently rolling prairie, with here and there patches of brush at the bottoms of the slopes around the dry watercourses.

At last we reached a somewhat deeper valley, in which the wolves were harbored. Wolves lie close in the daytime and will not leave cover if they can help it; and as they had both food and water within we knew it was most unlikely that this couple would be gone. The valley was a couple of hundred yards broad and three or four times as long, filled with a growth of ash and dwarf elm and cedar, thorny underbrush choking the spaces between. Posting the cowboy, to whom he gave his rifle, with two greyhounds on one side of the upper end, and old man Prindle with two others on the opposite side, while I was left at the lower end to guard against the possibility of the wolves breaking back, the Judge himself rode into the thicket near me and loosened the track-hounds to let them find the wolves' trial. The big dogs also were uncoupled and allowed to go in with the hounds. Their power of scent was very poor, but they were sure to be guided aright by the baying of the hounds, and their presence would give confidence to the latter and make them ready to rout the wolves out of the thicket, which they would probably have shrunk from doing alone. There was a moment's pause of expectation after the Judge entered the thicket with his hounds. We sat motionless on our horses, eagerly looking through the keen fresh morning air. Then a clamorous baying from the thicket in which both the horseman and dogs had disappeared showed that the hounds had struck the trail of their quarry and were running on a hot scent. For a couple of minutes we could not be quite certain which way the game was going to break. The hounds ran zigzag through the brush, as we could tell by their baying, and once some yelping and a great row showed that they had come rather closer than they had expected upon at least one of the wolves.

In another minute, however, the latter found it too hot for them and bolted from the thicket. My first notice of this was seeing the cowboy, who was standing by the side of his horse, suddenly throw up his rifle and fire, while the greyhounds who had been springing high in the air, half maddened by the clamor in the thicket below, for a moment dashed off the wrong way, confused by the report of the gun. I rode for all I was worth to where the cowboy stood, and instantly caught a glimpse of two wolves, grizzled-gray and brown, which, having been turned by his shot, had started straight over the hill across the plain toward the mountains three miles away. As soon as I saw them I also saw that the rearmost of the couple had been hit somewhere in the body and was lagging behind, the blood running from its flanks, while the two greyhounds were racing after it; and at the same moment the track-hounds and the big dogs burst out of the thicket, yelling savagely as they struck the bloody trail. The wolf was hard hit, and staggered as he ran. He did not have a hundred yards' start of the dogs, and in less than a minute one of the greyhounds ranged up and passed him with a savage snap that brought him to; and before he could recover the whole pack rushed at him. Weakened as he was he could make no effective fight against so many foes, and indeed had a chance for but one or two rapid snaps before he was thrown down and completely covered by the bodies of his enemies. Yet with one of these snaps he did damage, as a shrill yell told, and in a second an over-rash track-hound came out of the struggle with a deep gash across his shoulders. The worrying, growling, and snarling were terrific, but in a minute the heaving mass grew motionless and the dogs drew off save one or two that still continued to worry the dead wolf as it lay stark and stiff with glazed eyes and rumpled fur.

No sooner were we satisfied that it was dead than the Judge, with cheers and oaths and crackings of his whip, urged the dogs after the other wolf. The two greyhounds that had been with old man Prindle had fortunately not been able to see the wolves when they first broke from the cover, and never saw the wounded wolf at all, starting off at full speed after the unwounded one the instant he topped the crest of the hill. He had taken advantage of a slight hollow and turned, and now the chase was crossing us half a mile away. With whip and spur we flew toward them, our two greyhounds stretching out in front and leaving us as if we were standing still, the track-hounds and big dogs running after them just ahead of the horses. Fortunately the wolf plunged for a moment into a little brushy hollow and again doubled back, and this gave us a chance to see the end of the chase from nearby. The two greyhounds which had first taken up the pursuit were then but a short distance behind. Nearer they crept until they were within ten yards, and then with a tremendous race the little bitch ran past him and inflicted a vicious bite in the big beast's ham. He whirled around like a top and his jaws clashed like those of a sprung bear-trap, but quick though he was she was quicker and just cleared his savage rush. In another moment he resumed his flight at full speed, a speed which only that of the greyhounds exceeded; but almost immediately the second greyhound ranged alongside, and though he was not able to bite, because the wolf kept running with its head turned around threatening him, yet by his feints he delayed the beast's flight so that in a moment or two the remaining couple of swift hounds arrived on the scene. For a moment the wolf and all four dogs galloped along in a bunch; then one of the greyhounds, watching his chance, pinned the beast cleverly by the hock and threw him completely over. The others jumped on it in an instant; but rising by main strength the wolf shook himself free, catching one dog by the ear and tearing it half off. Then he sat down on his haunches and the greyhounds ranged themselves around him some twenty yards off, forming a ring which forbade his retreat, though they themselves did not dare touch him. However the end was at hand. In another moment Old Abe and General Grant came running up at headlong speed and smashed into the wolf like a couple of battering-rams. He rose on his hind-legs like a wrestler as they came at him, the greyhounds also rising and bouncing up and down like rubber balls. I could just see the wolf and the first big dog locked together, as the second one made good his throat-hold. In another moment over all three tumbled, while the greyhounds and one or two of the track-hounds jumped in to take part in the killing. The big dogs more than occupied the wolf's attention and took all the punishing, while in a trice one of the greyhounds, having seized him by the hind-leg, stretched him out, and the others were biting his undefended belly. The snarling and yelling of the worry made a noise so fiendish that it was fairly bloodcurdling; then it gradually died down, and the second wolf lay limp on the plain, killed by the dogs unassisted. This wolf was rather heavier and decidedly taller than either of the big dogs, with more sinewy feet and longer fangs.

I have several times seen wolves run down and stopped by greyhounds after a break-neck gallop and a wildly exciting finish, but this was the only occasion on which I ever saw the dogs kill a big full-grown he-wolf unaided. Nevertheless various friends of mine own packs that have performed the feat again and again. One pack, formerly kept at Fort Benton, until wolves in that neighborhood became scarce, had nearly seventy-five to its credit, most of them killed without any assistance from the hunter; killed moreover by the greyhounds alone, there being no other dogs with the pack. These greyhounds were trained to the throat-hold, and did their own killing in fine style; usually six or eight were slipped together. General Miles informs me that he once had great fun in the Indian Territory hunting wolves with a pack of greyhounds. They had with the pack a large stub-tailed mongrel, of doubtful ancestry but most undoubted fighting capacity. When the wolf was started the greyhounds were sure to overtake it in a mile or two; they would then bring it to a halt and stand around it in a ring until the fighting dog came up. The latter promptly tumbled on the wolf, grabbing him anywhere, and often getting a terrific wound himself at the same time. As soon as he had seized the wolf and was rolling over with him in the grapple the other dogs joined in the fray and despatched the quarry without much danger to themselves.

During the last decade many ranchmen in Colorado, Wyoming, and Montana have developed packs of greyhounds able to kill a wolf unassisted. Greyhounds trained for this purpose always seize by the throat; and the light dogs used for coursing jack-rabbits are not of much service, smooth or rough-haired greyhounds and deer-hounds standing over thirty inches at the shoulder and weighing over ninety pounds being the only ones that, together with speed, courage, and endurance, possess the requisite power.

One of the most famous packs in the West was that of the Sun River Hound Club, in Montana, started by the stockmen of Sun River to get rid of the curse of wolves which infested the neighborhood and worked very serious damage to the herds and flocks. The pack was composed of both greyhounds and deer-hounds, the best being from the kennels of Colonel Williams and of Mr. Van Hummel, of Denver; they were handled by an old plainsman and veteran wolf-hunter named Porter. In the season of '86 the astonishing number of 146 wolves were killed with these dogs. Ordinarily, as soon as the dogs seized a wolf, and threw or held it, Porter rushed in and stabbed it with his hunting-knife; one day, when out with six hounds, he thus killed no less than twelve out of the fifteen wolves started, though one of the greyhounds was killed, and all the others were cut and exhausted. But often the wolves were killed without his aid. The first time the two biggest hounds — deer-hounds or wire-haired grey-hounds — were tried, when they had been at the ranch only three days, they performed such a feat. A large wolf had killed and par-tially eaten a sheep in a corral close to the ranch house, and Porter started on the trail, and followed him at a jog-trot nearly ten miles before the hounds sighted him. Running but a few rods, he turned viciously to bay, and the two great greyhounds struck him like stones hurled from a catapult, throwing him as they fastened on his throat; they held him down and strangled him before he could rise, two other hounds getting up just in time to help at the end of the worry.

Ordinarily, however, no two greyhounds or deer-hounds are a match for a gray wolf, but I have known of several instances in Colorado, Wyoming, and Montana, in which three strong veter-ans have killed one. The feat can only be performed by big dogs of the highest courage, who all act together, rush in at top speed, and seize by the throat; for the strength of the quarry is such that otherwise he will shake off the dogs, and then speedily kill them by rapid snaps with his terribly armed jaws. Where possible, half a dozen dogs should be slipped at once, to minimize the risk of injury to the pack; unless this is done, and unless the hunter helps the dogs in the worry, accidents will be frequent and an occasional wolf will be found able to beat off, maiming or killing, a lesser number of assailants. Some hunters prefer the smooth greyhound, because of its great speed, and others the wire-coated animal, the rough deer-hound, because of its superior strength; both, if of the right kind, are dauntless fighters.

Colonel Williams' greyhounds have performed many noble feats in wolf-hunting. He spent the winter of 1875 in the Black Hills, which at that time did not contain a single settler and fairly swarmed with game. Wolves were especially numerous and very bold and fierce, so that the dogs of the party were continually in jeopardy of their lives. On the other hand they took an ample vengeance, for many wolves were caught by the pack. Whenever possible, the horsemen kept close enough to take an immediate hand in the fight, if the quarry was a full-grown wolf, and thus save the dogs from the terrible punishment they were otherwise certain to receive. The dogs invariably throttled, rushing straight at the throat, but the wounds they themselves received were generally in the flank or belly; in several instances these wounds resulted fatally. Once or twice a wolf was caught, and held by two greyhounds until the horsemen came up; but it took at least five dogs to overcome and slay unaided a big timber wolf. Several times the feat was performed by a party of five, consisting of two greyhounds, one rough-coated deer-hound, and two cross-bloods; and once by a litter of seven young greyhounds, not yet come to their full strength.

Once or twice the so-called Russian wolf-hounds or silky coated greyhounds, the "borzois," have been imported and tried in wolf-hunting on the Western plains; but hitherto they have not shown themselves equal, at either running or fighting, to the big American-bred greyhounds of the type produced by Colonel Williams and certain others of our best Western breeders. Indeed I have never known any foreign greyhounds, whether Scotch, English, or from Continental Europe, to perform such feats of courage, endurance, and strength, in chasing and killing dangerous game, as the home-bred greyhounds of Colonel Williams.

CHAPTER IX

IN COWBOY LAND

OUT on the frontier, and generally among those who spend their lives in, or on the borders of, the wilderness, life is reduced to its elemental conditions. The passions and emotions of these grim hunters of the mountains, and wild rough-riders of the plains, are simpler and stronger than those of people dwelling in more complicated states of society. As soon as the communities become settled and begin to grow with any rapidity, the American instinct for law asserts itself; but in the earlier stages each individual is obliged to be a law to himself and to guard his rights with a strong hand. Of course the transition periods are full of incongruities. Men have not yet adjusted their relations to morality and law with any niceness. They hold strongly by certain rude virtues, and on the other hand they quite fail to recognize even as shortcomings not a few traits that obtain scant mercy in older communities. Many of the desperadoes, the man-killers, and road-agents have good sides to their characters. Often they are people who, in certain stages of civilization, do, or have done, good work, but who, when these stages have passed, find themselves surrounded by conditions which accentuate their worst qualities, and make their best qualities useless. The average desperado, for instance, has, after all, much the same standard of morals that the Norman nobles had in the days of the battle of Hastings, and, ethically and morally, he is decidedly in advance of the vikings, who were the ancestors of these same nobles—and to whom, by the way, he himself could doubtless trace a portion of his blood. If the transition from the wild lawlessness of life in the wilderness or on the border to a higher civilization were stretched out over a term of centuries, he and his descendants would doubtless accommodate themselves by degrees to the changing circumstances. But unfortunately in the far West the transition takes place with marvelous abruptness, and at an altogether unheard-of speed, and many a man's nature is unable to change with sufficient rapidity to allow him to harmonize with his environment. In consequence, unless he leaves for still wilder lands, he ends by getting hanged instead of founding a family which would revere his name as that of a very capable, although not in all respects a conventionally moral, ancestor.

Most of the men with whom I was intimately thrown during my life on the frontier and in the wilderness were good fellows, hardworking, brave, resolute, and truthful. At times, of course, they were forced of necessity to do deeds which would seem startling to dwellers in cities and in old settled places; and though they waged a very stern and relentless warfare upon evil-doers whose misdeeds had immediate and tangible bad results, they showed a wide toleration of all save the most extreme classes of wrong, and were not given to inquiring too curiously into a strong man's past, or to criticizing him over-harshly for a failure to discriminate in finer ethical questions. Moreover, not a few of the men with whom I came in contact—with some of whom my relations were very close and friendly—had at different times led rather tough careers. This was accepted by them and by their companions as a fact, and—nothing more. There were certain offences, such as rape, the robbery of a friend, or murder under circumstances of cowardice and treachery, which were never forgiven; but the fact that when the country was wild a young fellow had gone on the road—that is, become a highwayman, or had been chief of a gang of desperadoes, horse-thieves, and cattle-killers—was scarcely held to weigh against him, being treated as a regrettable, but certainly not shameful, trait of youth. He was regarded by his neighbors with the same kindly tolerance which respectable mediæval Scotch borderers doubtless extended to their wilder young men who would persist in raiding English cattle even in time of peace.

Of course if these men were asked outright as to their stories they would have refused to tell them or else would have lied about them; but when they had grown to regard a man as a friend and companion they would often recount various incidents of their past lives with perfect frankness, and as they combined in a very curious degree both a decided sense of humor, and a failure to appreciate that there was anything especially remarkable in what they related, their tales were always entertaining.

Early one spring, now nearly ten years ago, I was out hunting some lost horses. They had strayed from the range three months before, and we had in a roundabout way heard that they were ranging near some broken country, where a man named Brophy had a ranch, nearly fifty miles from my own. When I started thither the weather was warm, but the second day out it grew colder and a heavy snowstorm came on. Fortunately I was able to reach the ranch all right, finding there one of the sons of a Little Beaver ranchman, and a young cowpuncher belonging to a Texas outfit, whom I knew very well. After putting my horse into the corral and throwing him down some hay I strode into the low hut, made partly of turf and partly of cottonwood logs, and speedily warmed myself before the fire. We had a good warm supper, of bread, potatoes, fried venison, and tea. My two companions grew very sociable and began to talk freely over their pipes. There were two bunks one above the other. I climbed into the upper, leaving my friends, who occupied the lower, sitting together on a bench recounting different incidents in the careers of themselves and their cronies during the winter that had just passed. Soon one of them asked the other what had become of a certain horse, a noted cutting pony, which I had myself noticed the preceding fall. The question aroused the other to the memory of a wrong which still rankled, and he began (I alter one or two of the proper names):

"Why, that was the pony that got stole. I had been workin' him on rough ground when I was out with the Three Bar outfit and he went tender forward, so I turned him loose by the Lazy B ranch, and when I came back to git him there wasn't anybody at the ranch and I couldn't find him. The sheep-man who lives about two miles west, under Red Clay butte, told me he seen a fellow in a wolfskin coat, ridin' a pinto bronco, with white eyes, leadin' that pony of mine just two days before; and I hunted round till I hit his trail and then I followed to where I'd reckoned he was headin' for— the Short Pine Hills. When I got there a rancher told me he had seen the man pass on towards Cedartown, and sure enough when I struck Cedartown I found he lived there in a 'dobe house, just outside the town. There was a boom on the town and it looked pretty slick. There was two hotels and I went into the first, and I says, 'Where's the justice of the peace?' says I to the bartender.

"'There ain't no justice of the peace,' says he, 'the justice of the peace got shot.'

" 'Well, where's the constable?' says I.

" 'Why, it was him that shot the justice of the peace!' says he; 'he's skipped the country with a bunch of horses.'

" 'Well, ain't there no officer of the law left in this town?' says I.

" 'Why, of course,' says he, 'there's a probate judge; he is over tendin' bar at the Last Chance Hotel.'

"So I went over to the Last Chance Hotel and I walked in there. 'Mornin',' says I.

" 'Mornin',' says he.

" 'You're the probate judge?' says I.

" 'That's what I am,' says he. 'What do you want?' says he.

" 'I want justice,' says I.

" 'What kind of justice do you want?' says he. 'What's it for?'

" 'It's for stealin' a horse,' says I.

" 'Then by God you'll git it,' says he. 'Who stole the horse?' says he.

" 'It is a man that lives in a 'dobe house, just outside the town there,' says I.

" 'Well, where do you come from yourself?' said he.

" 'From Medory,' said I.

"With that he lost interest and settled kind o' back, and says he, 'There won't no Cedartown jury hang a Cedartown man for stealin' a Medory man's horse,' said he.

" 'Well, what am I to do about my horse?' says I.

" 'Do?' says he; 'well, you know where the man lives, don't you?' says he; 'then sit up outside his house to-night and shoot him when he comes in,' says he, 'and skip out with the horse.'

" 'All right,' says I, 'that is what I'll do,' and I walked off.

"So I went off to his house and I laid down behind some sage-bushes to wait for him. He was not at home, but I could see his wife movin' about inside now and then, and I waited and waited, and it growed darker, and I begun to say to myself, 'Now here you are lyin' out to shoot this man when he comes home; and it's gettin' dark, and you don't know him, and if you do shoot the next man that comes into that house, like as not it won't be the fellow you're after at all, but some perfectly innocent man a-comin' there after the other man's wife!'

"So I up and saddled the bronc' and lit out for home," concluded the narrator with the air of one justly proud of his own self-abnegating virtue.

The "town" where the judge above-mentioned dwelt was one of those squalid pretentiously named little clusters of makeshift dwellings which on the edge of the wild country spring up with the rapid growth of mushrooms, and are often no longer lived. In their earlier stages these towns are frequently built entirely of canvas, and are subject to grotesque calamities. When the territory purchased from the Sioux, in the Dakotas, a couple of years ago, was thrown open to settlement there was a furious inrush of men on horseback and in wagons, and various ambitious cities sprang up overnight. The new settlers were all under the influence of that curious craze which causes every true Westerner to put unlimited faith in the unknown and untried; many had left all they had in a far better farming country, because they were true to their immemorial belief that, wherever they were, their luck would be better if they went somewhere else. They were always on the move, and headed for the vague beyond. As miners see visions of all the famous mines of history in each new camp, so these would-be city founders saw future St. Pauls and Omahas in every forlorn group of tents pitched by some muddy stream in a desert of gumbo and sage-brush; and they named both the towns and the canvas buildings in accordance with their bright hopes for the morrow, rather than with reference to the mean facts of the day. One of these towns, which when twenty-four hours old boasted of six saloons, a "court-house," and an "opera house," was overwhelmed by early disaster. The third day of its life a whirlwind came along and took off the opera house and half the saloons; and the following evening lawless men nearly finished the work of the elements. The riders of a huge trail-outfit from Texas, to their glad surprise discovered the town and abandoned themselves to a night of roaring and lethal carousal. Next morning the city authorities were lamenting, with oaths of bitter rage, that "them hell-and-twenty Flying A cowpunchers had cut the court-house up into pants." It was true. The cowboys were in need of chaps, and with an admirable mixture of adventurousness, frugality, and ready adaptability to circumstances, had made substitutes therefore in the shape of canvas overalls, cut from the roof and walls of the shaky temple of justice.

One of my valued friends in the mountains, and one of the best hunters with whom I ever traveled, was a man who had a peculiarly light-hearted way of looking at conventional social obligations. Though in some ways a true backwoods Donatello, he was a man of much shrewdness and of great courage and resolution. Moreover, he possessed what only a few men do possess, the capacity to tell the truth. He saw facts as they were, and could tell them as they were, and he never told an untruth unless for very weighty reasons. He was pre-eminently a philosopher, of a happy, sceptical turn of mind. He had no prejudices. He never looked down, as so many hard characters do, upon a person possessing a different code of ethics. His attitude was one of broad, genial tolerance. He saw nothing out of the way in the fact that he had himself been a road-agent, a professional gambler, and a desperado at different stages of his career. On the other hand, he did not in the least hold it against any one that he had always acted within the law. At the time that I knew him he had become a man of some substance, and naturally a stanch upholder of the existing order of things. But while he never boasted of his past deeds, he never apologized for them, and evidently would have been quite as incapable of understanding that they needed an apology as he would have been incapable of being guilty of mere vulgar boastfulness. He did not often allude to his past career at all. When he did, he recited its incidents perfectly naturally and simply, as events, without any reference to or regard for their ethical significance. It was this quality which made him at times a specially pleasant companion, and always an agreeable narrator. The point of his story, or what seemed to him the point, was rarely that which struck me. It was the incidental sidelights the story threw upon his own nature and the somewhat lurid surroundings amid which he had moved.

On one occasion when we were out together we killed a bear, and after skinning it, took a bath in a lake. I noticed he had a scar on the side of his foot and asked him how he got it, to which he responded, with indifference:

"Oh, that? Why, a man shootin' at me to make me dance, that was all."

I expressed some curiosity in the matter, and he went on:

"Well, the way of it was this: It was when I was keeping a saloon in New Mexico, and there was a man there by the name of Fowler, and there was a reward on him of three thousand dollars — "

"Put on him by the state?"

"No, put on by his wife," said my friend; "and there was this — "

"Hold on," I interrupted; "put on by his wife did you say?"

"Yes, by his wife. Him and her had been keepin' a faro bank, you see, and they quarreled about it, so she just put a reward on him, and so — "

"Excuse me," I said, "but do you mean to say that this reward was put on publicly?" to which my friend answered, with an air of gentlemanly boredom at being interrupted to gratify my thirst for irrelevant detail:

"Oh, no, not publicly. She just mentioned it to six or eight intimate personal friends."

"Go on," I responded, somewhat overcome by this instance of the primitive simplicity with which New Mexican matrimonial disputes were managed, and he continued:

"Well, two men come ridin' in to see me to borrow my guns. My guns was Colt's self-cockers. It was a new thing then, and they was the only ones in town. These come to me, and 'Simpson,' says they, 'we want to borrow your guns; we are goin' to kill Fowler.'

"'Hold on for a moment,' said I, 'I am willin' to lend you them guns, but I ain't goin' to know what you 'r' goin' to do with them, no sir; but of course you can have the guns.'" Here my friend's face lightened pleasantly, and he continued:

"Well, you may easily believe I felt surprised next day when Fowler come ridin' in, and, says he, 'Simpson, here's your guns!' He had shot them two men! 'Well, Fowler,' says I, 'if I had known them men was after you, I'd never have let them have them guns nohow,' says I. That wasn't true, for I did know it, but there was no cause to tell him that." I murmured my approval of such prudence, and Simpson continued, his eyes gradually brightening with the light of agreeable reminiscence:

"Well, they up and they took Fowler before the justice of the peace. The justice of the peace was a Turk."

"Now, Simpson, what do you mean by that?" I interrupted.

"Well, he come from Turkey," said Simpson, and I again sank back, wondering briefly what particular variety of Mediterranean outcast had drifted down to Mexico to be made a justice of the peace. Simpson laughed and continued: "That Fowler was a funny fellow. The Turk, he committed Fowler, and Fowler, he riz up and knocked him down and tromped all over him and made him let him go!"

"That was an appeal to a higher law," I observed. Simpson assented cheerily, and continued:

"Well, that Turk, he got nervous for fear Fowler he was goin' to kill him, and so he comes to me and offers me twenty-five dollars a day to protect him from Fowler; and I went to Fowler, and 'Fowler,' says I, 'that Turk 's offered me twenty-five dollars a day to protect him from you. Now, I ain't goin' to get shot for no twenty-five dollars a day, and if you are goin' to kill the Turk, just say so and go and do it; but if you ain't goin' to kill the Turk, there's no reason why I shouldn't earn that twenty-five dollars a day!' and Fowler, says he, 'I ain't goin' to touch the Turk; you just go right ahead and protect him.'"

So Simpson "protected" the Turk from the imaginary danger of Fowler, for about a week, at twenty-five dollars a day. Then one evening he happened to go out and met Fowler, "and," said he, "the moment I saw him I know he felt mean, for he begun to shoot at my feet," which certainly did seem to offer presumptive evidence of meanness. Simpson continued:

"I didn't have no gun, so I just had to stand there and take it until something distracted his attention, and I went off home to get my gun and kill him, but I wanted to do it perfectly lawful; so I went up to the mayor (he was playin' poker with one of the judges), and says I to him, 'Mr. Mayor,' says I, 'I am goin' to shoot Fowler.' And the mayor he riz out of his chair and he took me by the hand, and says he, 'Mr. Simpson, if you do I will stand by you;' and the judge, he says, 'I'll go on your bond.'"

Fortified by this cordial approval of the executive and judicial branches of the government, Mr. Simpson started on his quest. Meanwhile, however, Fowler had cut up another prominent citizen, and they already had him in jail. The friends of law and order feeling some little distrust as to the permanency of their own zeal for righteousness, thought it best to settle the matter before there was time for cooling, and accordingly, headed by Simpson, the mayor, the judge, the Turk, and other prominent citizens of the town, they broke into the jail and hanged Fowler. The point in the hanging which especially tickled my friend's fancy as he lingered over the reminiscence, was one that was rather too ghastly to appeal to our own sense of humor. In the Turk's mind there still rankled the memory of Fowler's very unprofessional conduct while figuring before him as a criminal. Said Simpson, with a merry twinkle of the eye: "Do you know that Turk, he was a right funny fellow too after all. Just as the boys were going to string up Fowler, says he, 'Boys, stop; one moment, gentlemen, — Mr. Fowler, good-by,' and he blew a kiss to him!"

In the cow-country, and elsewhere on the wild borderland between savagery and civilization, men go quite as often by nicknames as by those to which they are lawfully entitled. Half the cowboys and hunters of my acquaintance are known by names entirely unconnected with those they inherited or received when they were christened. Occasionally some would-be desperado or make-believe mighty hunter tries to adopt what he deems a title suitable to his prowess; but such an effort is never attempted in really wild places, where it would be greeted with huge derision; for all of these names that are genuine are bestowed by outsiders, with small regard to the wishes of the person named. Ordinarily the name refers to some easily recognizable accident of origin, occupation, or aspect; as witness the innumerable Dutcheys, Frencheys, Kentucks, Texas Jacks, Bronco Bills, Bear Joes, Buckskins, Red Jims, and the like. Sometimes it is apparently meaningless; one of my cow-puncher friends is always called "Sliver" or "Splinter" — why, I have no idea. At other times some particular incident may give rise to the title: a clean-looking cowboy formerly in my employ was always known as "Muddy Bill," because he had once been bucked off his horse into a mud hole.

The grewsome genesis of one such name is given in the following letter which I have just received from an old hunting-friend in the Rockies, who took a kindly interest in a frontier cabin which the Boone and Crockett Club was putting up at the Chicago World's Fair.

"Feb 16th 1893; Der Sir: I see in the newspapers that your club the Daniel Boon and Davey Crockit you Intend to erect a fruntier Cabin at the world's Far at Chicago to represent the erley Pianears of our country I would like to see you maik a success I have all my life been a fruntiersman and feel interested in your undertaking and I hoap you wile get a good assortment of relicks I want to maik one suggestion to you that is in regard to geting a good man and a genuine Mauntanner to take charg of your haus at Chicago I want to recommend a man for you to get it is Liver-eating Johnson that is the naim he is generally called he is an olde mauntneer and large and fine looking and one of the Best Story Tellers in the country and Very Polight genteel to every one he meets I wil tel you how he got that naim Liver-eating in a hard Fight with the Black Feet Indians thay Faught all day Johnson and a few Whites Faught a large Body of Indians all day after the fight Johnson cam in contact with a wounded Indian and Johnson was aut of ammunition and thay faught it out with thar Knives and Johnson got away with the Indian and in the fight cut the livver out of the Indian and said to the Boys did thay want any Liver to eat that is the way he got the naim of Liver-eating Johnson

"Yours truly" etc., etc.

Frontiersmen are often as original in their theories of life as in their names; and the originality may take the form of wild savagery, of mere uncouthness, or of an odd combination of genuine humor with simple acceptance of facts as they are. On one occasion I expressed some surprise at learning that a certain Mrs. P. had suddenly married, though her husband was alive and in jail in a neighboring town; and received for answer: "Well, you see, old man Pete he skipped the country, and left his widow behind him, and so Bob Evans he up and married her!"—which was evidently felt to be a proceeding requiring no explanation whatever.

In the cow-country there is nothing more refreshing than the light-hearted belief entertained by the average man to the effect that any animal which by main force has been saddled and ridden, or harnessed and driven a couple of times, is a "broke horse." My present foreman is firmly wedded to this idea, as well as to its complement, the belief that any animal with hoofs, before any vehicle with wheels, can be driven across any country. One summer on reaching the ranch I was entertained with the usual accounts of the adventures and misadventures which had befallen my own men and my neighbors since I had been out last. In the course of the conversation my foreman remarked: "We had a great time out here about six weeks ago. There was a professor from Ann Arbor came out with his wife to see the Bad Lands, and they asked if we could rig them up a team, and we said we guessed we could, and Foley's boy and I did; but it ran away with him and broke his leg! He was here for a month. I guess he didn't mind it though." Of this I was less certain, forlorn little Medora being a "busted" cow-town, concerning which I once heard another of my men remark, in reply to an inquisitive commercial traveler: "How many people lives here? Eleven—counting the chickens—when they're all in town!"

My foreman continued: "By George, there was something that professor said afterward that made me feel hot. I sent word up to him by Foley's boy that seein' as how it had come out we would n't charge him nothin' for the rig; and that professor he answered that he was glad we were showing him some sign of consideration, for he'd begun to believe he'd fallen into a den of sharks, and that we gave him a runaway team a purpose. That made me hot, calling that a runaway team. Why, there was one of them horses never *could* have run away before; it had n't never been druv but twice! and the other horse maybe had run away a few times, but there was lots of times he *had n't* run away. I esteemed that team full as liable not to run away as it was to run away," concluded my foreman, evidently deeming this as good a warranty of gentleness in a horse as the most exacting could possibly require.

The definition of good behavior on the frontier is even more elastic for a saddle-horse than for a team. Last spring one of the Three-Seven riders, a magnificent horseman, was killed on the round-up near Belfield, his horse bucking and falling on him. "It was accounted a plumb gentle horse too," said my informant, "only it sometimes sulked and acted a little mean when it was cinched up behind." The unfortunate rider did not know of this failing of the "plumb gentle horse," and as soon as he was in the saddle it threw itself over sideways with a great bound, and he fell on his head, and never spoke again.

Such accidents are too common in the wild country to attract very much attention; the men accept them with grim quiet, as inevitable in such lives as theirs—lives that are harsh and narrow in their toil and their pleasure alike, and that are ever-bounded by an iron horizon of hazard and hardship. During the last year and a half three other men from the ranches in my immediate neighborhood have met their deaths in the course of their work. One, a trail boss of the O X, was drowned while swimming his herd across a swollen river. Another, one of the fancy ropers of the W Bar, was killed while roping cattle in a corral; his saddle turned, the rope twisted round him, he was pulled off, and was trampled to death by his own horse.

The fourth man, a cowpuncher named Hamilton, lost his life during the last week of October, 1891, in the first heavy snow-storm of the season. Yet he was a skilled plainsman, on ground he knew well, and just before straying himself, he successfully instructed two men who did not know the country how to get to camp. They were all three with the round-up, and were making a circle through the Bad Lands; the wagons had camped on the eastern edge of these Bad Lands, where they merged into the prairie, at the head of an old disused road, which led about due east from the Little Missouri. It was a gray, lowering day, and as darkness came on Hamilton's horse played out, and he told his two companions not to wait, as it had begun to snow, but to keep on toward the north, skirting some particularly rough buttes, and as soon as they struck the road to turn to the right and follow it out to the prairie, where they would find camp; he particularly warned them to keep a sharp lookout, so as not to pass over the dim trail unawares in the dusk and the storm. They followed his advice, and reached camp safely; and after they had left him nobody ever again saw him alive. Evidently he himself, plodding northward, passed over the road without seeing it in the gathering gloom; probably he struck it at some point where the ground was bad, and the dim trail in consequence disappeared entirely, as is the way with these prairie roads—making them landmarks to be used with caution. He must then have walked on and on, over rugged hills and across deep ravines, until his horse came to a standstill; he took off its saddle and picketed it to a dwarfed ash. Its frozen carcass was found with the saddle near by, two months later. He now evidently recognized some landmark, and realized that he had passed the road, and was far to the north of the round-up wagons; but he was a resolute, self-confident man, and he determined to strike out for a line camp, which he knew lay about due east of him, two or three miles out on the prairie, on one of the head branches of Knife River. Night must have fallen by this time, and he missed the camp, probably passing it within less than a mile; but he did pass it, and with it all hopes of life, and walked wearily on to his doom, through the thick darkness and the driving snow. At last his strength failed, and he lay down in the tall grass of a little hollow. Five months later, in the early spring, the riders from the line camp found his body, resting face downward, with the forehead on the folded arms.

Accidents of less degree are common. Men break their collar-bones, arms, or legs by falling when riding at speed over dangerous ground, when cutting cattle or trying to control a stampeded herd, or by being thrown or rolled on by bucking or rearing horses; or their horses, and on rare occasions even they themselves, are gored by fighting steers. Death by storm or in flood, death in striving to master a wild and vicious horse, or in handling maddened cattle, and too often death in brutal conflict with one of his own fellows—any one of these is the not unnatural end of the life of the dweller on the plains or in the mountains.

But a few years ago other risks had to be run from savage beasts, and from the Indians. Since I have been ranching on the Little Missouri, two men have been killed by bears in the neighborhood of my range; and in the early years of my residence there, several men living or traveling in the country were slain by small war-parties of young braves. All the old-time trappers and hunters could tell stirring tales of their encounters with Indians.

My friend, Tazewell Woody, was among the chief actors in one of the most noteworthy adventures of this kind. He was a very quiet man, and it was exceedingly difficult to get him to talk over any of his past experiences; but one day, when he was in high good-humor with me for having made three consecutive straight shots at elk, he became quite communicative, and I was able to get him to tell me one story which I had long wished to hear from his lips, having already heard of it through one of the other survivors of the incident. When he found that I already knew a good deal old Woody told me the rest.

It was in the spring of 1875, and Woody and two friends were trapping on the Yellowstone. The Sioux were very bad at the time and had killed many prospectors, hunters, cowboys, and settlers; the whites retaliated whenever they got a chance, but, as always in Indian warfare, the sly, lurking, bloodthirsty savages inflicted much more loss than they suffered.

The three men, having a dozen horses with them, were camped by the river side in a triangular patch of brush, shaped a good deal like a common flatiron. On reaching camp they started to put out their traps; and when he came back in the evening Woody informed his companions that he had seen a great deal of Indian sign, and that he believed there were Sioux in the neighborhood. His companions both laughed at him, assuring him that they were not Sioux at all but friendly Crows, and that they would be in camp next morning; "and sure enough," said Woody, meditatively, "they *were* in camp next morning." By dawn one of the men went down the river to look at some of the traps, while Woody started out to where the horses were, the third man remaining in camp to get breakfast. Suddenly two shots were heard down the river, and in another moment a mounted Indian swept toward the horses. Woody fired, but missed him, and he drove off five while Woody, running forward, succeeded in herding the other seven into camp. Hardly had this been accomplished before the man who had gone down the river appeared, out of breath with his desperate run, having been surprised by several Indians, and just succeeding in making his escape by dodging from bush to bush, threatening his pursuers with his rifle.

These proved to be but the forerunners of a great war party, for when the sun rose the hills around seemed black with Sioux. Had they chosen to dash right in on the camp, running the risk of losing several of their men in the charge, they could of course have eaten up the three hunters in a minute; but such a charge is rarely practiced by Indians, who, although they are admirable in defensive warfare, and even in certain kinds of offensive movements, and although from their skill in hiding they usually inflict much more loss than they suffer when matched against white troops, are yet very reluctant to make any movement where the advantage gained must be offset by considerable loss of life. The three men thought they were surely doomed, but being veteran frontiersmen and long inured to every kind of hardship and danger, they set to work with cool resolution to make as effective a defense as possible, to beat off their antagonists if they might, and if this proved impracticable, to sell their lives as dearly as they could. Having tethered the horses in a slight hollow, the only one which offered any protection, each man crept out to a point of the triangular brush patch and lay down to await events.

In a very short while the Indians began closing in on them, taking every advantage of cover, and then, both from their side of the river and from the opposite bank, opened a perfect fusillade, wasting their cartridges with a recklessness which Indians are apt to show when excited. The hunters could hear the hoarse commands of the chiefs, the war-whoops and the taunts in broken English which some of the warriors hurled at them. Very soon all of their

horses were killed, and the brush was fairly riddled by the incessant volleys; but the three men themselves, lying flat on the
ground and well concealed, were not harmed. The more daring
young warriors then began to creep toward the hunters, going
stealthily from one piece of cover to the next; and now the whites
in turn opened fire. They did not shoot recklessly, as did their
foes, but coolly and quietly, endeavoring to make each shot tell.
Said Woody: "I only fired seven times all day; I reckoned on getting meat every time I pulled trigger." They had an immense
advantage over their enemies, in that whereas they lay still and
entirely concealed, the Indians of course had to move from cover
to cover in order to approach, and so had at times to expose themselves. When the whites fired at all they fired at a man, whether
moving or motionless, whom they could clearly see, while the
Indians could only shoot at the smoke, which imperfectly marked
the position of their unseen foes. In consequence the assailants
speedily found that it was a task of hopeless danger to try in such a
manner to close in on three plains veterans, men of iron nerve
and skilled in the use of the rifle. Yet some of the more daring
crept up very close to the patch of brush, and one actually got
inside of it, and was killed among the bedding that lay by the
smoldering camp-fire. The wounded and such of the dead as did
not lie in too exposed positions were promptly taken away by their
comrades; but seven bodies fell into the hands of the three
hunters. I asked Woody how many he himself had killed. He said
he could only be sure of two that he got; one he shot in the head
as he peeped over a bush, and the other he shot through the
smoke as he attempted to rush in. "My, how that Indian did yell,"
said Woody retrospectively, "*he* was no great of a stoic." After two or
three hours of this deadly skirmishing, which resulted in nothing
more serious to the whites than in two of them being slightly
wounded, the Sioux became disheartened by the loss they were
suffering and withdrew, confining themselves thereafter to a long
range and harmless fusillade. When it was dark the three men
crept out to the river bed, and taking advantage of the pitchy

night broke through the circle of their foes; they managed to reach the settlements without further molestation, having lost everything except their rifles.

For many years one of the most important of the wilderness dwellers was the West Point officer, and no man has played a greater part than he in the wild warfare which opened the regions beyond the Mississippi to white settlement. Since 1879, there has been but little regular Indian fighting in the North, though there have been one or two very tedious and wearisome campaigns waged against the Apaches in the South. Even in the North, however, there have been occasional uprisings which had to be quelled by the regular troops.

After my elk hunt in September, 1891, I came out through the Yellowstone Park, as I have elsewhere related, riding in company with a surveyor of the Burlington and Quincy railroad, who was just coming in from his summer's work. It was the first of October. There had been a heavy snow-storm and the snow was still falling. Riding a stout pony each, and leading another packed with our bedding, etc., we broke our way from the upper to the middle geyser basin. Here we found a troop of the 1st Cavalry camped, under the command of old friends of mine, Captain Frank Edwards and Lieutenant (now Captain) John Pitcher. They gave us hay for our horses and insisted upon our stopping to lunch, with the ready hospitality always shown by army officers. After lunch we began exchanging stories. My traveling companion, the surveyor, had that spring performed a feat of note, going through one of the canyons of the Big Horn for the first time. He went with an old mining inspector, the two of them dragging a cottonwood sledge over the ice. The walls of the canyon are so sheer and the water is so rough that it can be descended only when the stream is frozen. However, after six days' labor and hardship the descent was accomplished; and the surveyor, in concluding, described his experience in going through the Crow Reservation.

This turned the conversation upon Indians, and it appeared that both of our hosts had been actors in Indian scrapes which had attracted my attention at the time they occurred, as they took

place among tribes that I knew and in a country which I had some-
time visited, either when hunting or when purchasing horses for
the ranch. The first, which occurred to Captain Edwards, happened late in 1886, at the time when the Crow Medicine Chief,
Sword-Bearer, announced himself as the Messiah of the Indian
race, during one of the usual epidemics of ghost dancing. Sword-
Bearer derived his name from always wearing a medicine sword—
that is, a sabre painted red. He claimed to possess magic power,
and, thanks to the performance of many dexterous feats of jug-
gling, and the lucky outcome of certain prophecies, he deeply
stirred the Indians, arousing the young warriors in particular to
the highest pitch of excitement. They became sullen, began to
paint, and armed themselves; and the agent and the settlers
nearby grew so apprehensive that the troops were ordered to go to
the reservation. A body of cavalry, including Captain Edwards'
troop, was accordingly marched thither, and found the Crow warriors, mounted on their war ponies and dressed in their striking
battle-garb, waiting upon a hill.

The position of troops at the beginning of such an affair is
always peculiarly difficult. The settlers round about are sure to
clamor bitterly against them, no matter what they do, on the
ground that they are not thorough enough and are showing favor
to the savages, while on the other hand, even if they fight purely in
self-defense, a large number of worthy but weak-minded senti-
mentalists in the East are sure to shriek about their having brutally
attacked the Indians. The war authorities always insist that they
must not fire the first shot under any circumstances, and such
were the orders at this time. The Crows on the hilltop showed a
sullen and threatening front, and the troops advanced slowly
toward them and then halted for a parley.

Meanwhile a mass of black thunderclouds gathering on the
horizon threatened one of those cloudbursts of extreme severity
and suddenness so characteristic of the plains country. While still
trying to make arrangements for a parley, a horseman started out
of the Crow ranks and galloped headlong down toward the troops.

It was the medicine chief, Sword-Bearer. He was painted and in his battle-dress, wearing his war-bonnet of floating, trailing eagle feathers, while the plumes of the same bird were braided in the mane and tail of his fiery little horse. On he came at a gallop almost up to the troops and then began to circle around them, calling and singing and throwing his crimson sword into the air, catching it by the hilt as it fell. Twice he rode completely around the soldiers who stood in uncertainty, not knowing what to make of his performance, and expressly forbidden to shoot at him. Then paying no further heed to them he rode back toward the Crows. It appears that he had told them that he would ride twice around the hostile force, and by his incantations would call down rain from heaven, which would make the hearts of the white men like water, so that they should go back to their homes. Sure enough, while the arrangements for the parley were still going forward, down came the cloudburst, drenching the command and making the ground on the hills in front nearly impassable; and before it had dried a courier arrived with orders to the troops to go back to camp.

This fulfillment of Sword-Bearer's prophecy of course raised his reputation to the zenith and the young men of the tribe prepared for war, while the older chiefs, who more fully realized the power of the whites, still hung back. When the troops next appeared they came upon the entire Crow force, the women and children with their tepees being off to one side beyond a little stream while almost all the warriors of the tribe were gathered in front.

Sword-Bearer then started to repeat his former ride, to the intense irritation of the soldiers. Luckily, however, this time some of his young men could not be restrained. They too began to ride near the troops, and one of them was unable to refrain from firing on Captain Edwards' troop, which was in the van. This gave the soldiers their chance. They instantly responded with a volley, and Captain Edwards' troop charged. The fight lasted but a minute or two, for Sword-Bearer was struck by a bullet and fell, and as he had boasted himself invulnerable, and promised that his warriors should be invulnerable also if they would follow him, the hearts of the latter became as water and they broke in every direction. One of the amusing, though irritating, incidents of the affair was to see the plumed and painted warriors race headlong for the camp, plunge into the stream, wash off their war paint, and remove their feathers; in another moment they would be stolidly sitting on the ground, with their blankets over their shoulders, rising to greet the pursuing cavalry with unmoved composure and calm assurances that they had always been friendly and had much disapproved the conduct of the young bucks who had just been scattered on the field outside. It was much to the credit of the discipline of the army that no bloodshed followed the fight proper. The loss to the whites was small.

The other incident, related by Lieutenant Pitcher, took place, in 1890, near Tongue River, in northern Wyoming. The command with which he was serving was camped near the Cheyenne Reservation. One day two young Cheyenne bucks, met one of the government herders, and promptly killed him—in a sudden fit, half of ungovernable blood lust, half of mere ferocious lightheartedness. They then dragged his body into the brush and left it. The disappearance of the herder of course attracted attention, and a search was organized by the cavalry. At first the Indians stoutly denied all knowledge of the missing man; but when it became evident that the search party would shortly find him, two or three of the chiefs joined them, and piloted them to where the body lay; and acknowledged that he had been murdered by two of their band, though at first they refused to give their names. The commander of the post demanded that the murderers be given up.

The chiefs said that they were very sorry, that this could not be done, but that they were willing to pay over any reasonable number of ponies to make amends for the death. This offer was of course promptly refused, and the commander notified them that if they did not surrender the murderers by a certain time he would hold the whole tribe responsible and would promptly move out and attack them. Upon this the chiefs, after holding full counsel with the tribe, told the commander that they had no power to sur-render the murderers, but that the latter had said that sooner than see their tribe involved in a hopeless struggle they would of their own accord come in and meet the troops anywhere the latter chose to appoint, and die fighting. To this the commander responded: "All right; let them come into the agency in half an hour." The chiefs acquiesced, and withdrew.

Immediately the Indians sent mounted messengers at speed from camp to camp, summoning all their people to witness the act of fierce self-doom; and soon the entire tribe of Cheyennes, many of them having their faces blackened in token of mourn-ing, moved down and took up a position on the hillside close to the agency. At the appointed hour both young men appeared in their handsome war dress, galloped to the top of the hill near the encampment, and deliberately opened fire on the troops. The latter merely fired a few shots to keep the young despera-does off, while Lieutenant Pitcher and a score of cavalrymen left camp to make a circle and drive them in; they did not wish to hurt them, but to capture and give them over to the Indians, so that the latter might be forced themselves to inflict the punish-ment. However, they were unable to accomplish their purpose; one of the young braves went straight at them, firing his rifle and wounding the horse of one of the cavalrymen, so that, simply in self-defense, the latter had to fire a volley, which laid low the assailant; the other, his horse having been shot, was killed in the brush, fighting to the last. All the while, from the moment the two doomed braves appeared until they fell, the Cheyennes on the hillside had been steadily singing the death chant. When the young men had both died, and had thus averted the fate which their misdeeds would else have brought upon the tribe, the war-riors took their bodies and bore them away for burial honors, the soldiers looking on in silence. Where the slain men were buried the whites never knew; but all that night they listened to the dismal wailing of the dirges with which the tribesmen celebrated their gloomy funeral rites.

Frontiersmen are not, as a rule, apt to be very superstitious. They lead lives too hard and practical, and have too little imagination in things spiritual and supernatural. I have heard but few ghost stories while living on the frontier, and these few were of a perfectly commonplace and conventional type.

But I once listened to a goblin story which rather impressed me. It was told by a grisled, weatherbeaten old mountain hunter, named Bauman, who was born and had passed all his life on the frontier. He must have believed what he said, for he could hardly repress a shudder at certain points of the tale; but he was of German ancestry, and in childhood had doubtless been saturated with all kinds of ghost and goblin lore, so that many fearsome superstitions were latent in his mind; besides, he knew well the stories told by the Indian medicine men in their winter camps, of the snow-walkers, and the spectres, and the formless evil beings that haunt the forest depths, and dog and waylay the lonely wanderer who after nightfall passes through the regions where they lurk; and it may be that when overcome by the horror of the fate that befell his friend, and when oppressed by the awful dread of the unknown, he grew to attribute, both at the time and still more in remembrance, weird and elfin traits to what was merely some abnormally wicked and cunning wild beast; but whether this was so or not, no man can say.

When the event occurred Bauman was still a young man, and was trapping with a partner among the mountains dividing the forks of the Salmon from the head of Wisdom River. Not having had much luck, he and his partner determined to go up into a particularly wild and lonely pass through which ran a small stream said to contain many beaver. The pass had an evil reputation because the year before a solitary hunter who had wandered into it was there slain, seemingly by a wild beast, the half-eaten remains being afterward found by some mining prospectors who had passed his camp only the night before.

The memory of this event, however, weighed very lightly with the two trappers, who were as adventurous and hardy as others of their kind. They took their two lean mountain ponies to the foot of the pass, where they left them in an open beaver meadow, the rocky timber-clad ground being from thence onward impracticable for horses. They then struck out on foot through the vast, gloomy forest, and in about four hours reached a little open glade where they concluded to camp, as signs of game were plenty.

There was still an hour or two of daylight left, and after building a brush lean-to and throwing down and opening their packs, they started up stream. The country was very dense and hard to travel through, as there was much down timber, although here and there the sombre woodland was broken by small glades of mountain grass.

At dusk they again reached camp. The glade in which it was pitched was not many yards wide, the tall, close-set pines and firs rising round it like a wall. On one side was a little stream, beyond which rose the steep mountain-slopes, covered with the unbroken growth of the evergreen forest.

They were surprised to find that during their short absence something, apparently a bear, had visited camp, and had rummaged about among their things, scattering the contents of their packs, and in sheer wantonness destroying their lean-to. The footprints of the beast were quite plain, but at first they paid no particular heed to them, busying themselves with rebuilding the lean-to, laying out their beds and stores, and lighting the fire.

While Bauman was making ready supper, it being already dark, his companion began to examine the tracks more closely, and soon took a brand from the fire to follow them up, where the intruder had walked along a game trail after leaving the camp. When the brand flickered out, he returned and took another, repeating his inspection of the footprints very closely. Coming back to the fire, he stood by it a minute or two, peering out into the darkness, and suddenly remarked: "Bauman, that bear has been walking on two legs." Bauman laughed at this, but his partner insisted that he was right, and upon again examining the tracks with a torch, they certainly did seem to be made by but two paws, or feet. However, it was too dark to make sure. After discussing whether the footprints could possibly be those of a human being, and coming to the conclusion that they could not be, the two men rolled up in their blankets, and went to sleep under the lean-to.

At midnight Bauman was awakened by some noise, and sat up in his blankets. As he did so his nostrils were struck by a strong, wild-beast odor, and he caught the loom of a great body in the darkness at the mouth of the lean-to.

Grasping his rifle, he fired at the vague, threatening shadow, but must have missed, for immediately afterward he heard the smashing of the underwood as the thing, whatever it was, rushed off into the impenetrable blackness of the forest and the night.

After this the two men slept but little, sitting up by the rekindled fire, but they heard nothing more. In the morning they started out to look at the few traps they had set the previous evening and to put out new ones. By an unspoken agreement they kept together all day, and returned to camp toward evening.

On nearing it they saw, hardly to their astonishment, that the lean-to had been again torn down. The visitor of the preceding day had returned, and in wanton malice had tossed about their camp kit and bedding, and destroyed the shanty. The ground was marked up by its tracks, and on leaving the camp it had gone along the soft earth by the brook, where the footprints were as plain as if on snow, and, after a careful scrutiny of the trail, it certainly did seem as if, whatever the thing was, it had walked off on but two legs.

The men, thoroughly uneasy, gathered a great heap of dead logs, and kept up a roaring fire throughout the night, one or the other sitting on guard most of the time. About midnight the thing came down through the forest opposite, across the brook, and stayed there on the hillside for nearly an hour. They could hear the branches crackle as it moved about, and several times it uttered a harsh, grating, long-drawn moan, a peculiarly sinister sound. Yet it did not venture near the fire.

In the morning the two trappers, after discussing the strange events of the last thirty-six hours, decided that they would shoulder their packs and leave the valley that afternoon. They were the more ready to do this because in spite of seeing a good deal of game sign they had caught very little fur. However, it was necessary first to go along the line of their traps and gather them, and this they started out to do.

All the morning they kept together, picking up trap after trap, each one empty. On first leaving camp they had the disagreeable sensation of being followed. In the dense spruce thickets they occasionally heard a branch snap after they had passed; and now and then there were slight rustling noises among the small pines to one side of them.

At noon they were back within a couple of miles of camp. In the high, bright sunlight their fears seemed absurd to the two armed men, accustomed as they were, through long years of lonely wandering in the wilderness, to face every kind of danger from man, brute, or element. There were still three beaver traps to collect from a little pond in a wide ravine near by. Bauman volunteered to gather these and bring them in, while his companion went ahead to camp to make ready the packs.

On reaching the pond Bauman found three beaver in the traps, one of which had been pulled loose and carried into a beaver house. He took several hours in securing and preparing the beaver, and when he started homeward he marked with some uneasiness how low the sun was getting. As he hurried toward camp, under the tall trees, the silence and desolation of the forest weighed on him. His feet made no sound on the pine needles, and the slanting sun rays, striking through among the straight trunks, made a gray twilight in which objects at a distance glimmered indistinctly. There was nothing to break the ghostly stillness which, when there is no breeze, always broods over these sombre primeval forests.

At last he came to the edge of the little glade where the camp lay, and shouted as he approached it, but got no answer. The camp fire had gone out, though the thin blue smoke was still curling upward. Near it lay the packs, wrapped and arranged. At first Bauman could see nobody; nor did he receive an answer to his call. Stepping forward he again shouted, and as he did so his eye fell on the body of his friend, stretched beside the trunk of a great fallen spruce. Rushing toward it the horrified trapper found that the body was still warm, but that the neck was broken, while there were four great fang marks in the throat.

The footprints of the unknown beast-creature, printed deep in the soft soil, told the whole story.

The unfortunate man, having finished his packing, had sat down on the spruce log with his face to the fire, and his back to the dense woods, to wait for his companion. While thus waiting, his monstrous assailant, which must have been lurking nearby in the woods, waiting for a chance to catch one of the adventurers unprepared, came silently up from behind, walking with long, noiseless steps, and seemingly still on two legs. Evidently unheard, it reached the man, and broke his neck by wrenching his head back with its forepaws, while it buried its teeth in his throat. It had not eaten the body, but apparently had romped and gamboled round it in uncouth, ferocious glee, occasionally rolling over and over it; and had then fled back into the soundless depths of the woods.

Bauman, utterly unnerved, and believing that the creature with which he had to deal was something either half human or half devil, some great goblin-beast, abandoned everything but his rifle and struck off at speed down the pass, not halting until he reached the beaver meadows where the hobbled ponies were still grazing. Mounting, he rode onward through the night, until far beyond the reach of pursuit.

ENDNOTES

CHAPTER III

[1] Both this huge Alaskan bear and the entirely distinct bear of the barren grounds differ widely from the true grisly, at least in their extreme forms.

CHAPTER VII

[1] It is, however, quite possible, now that Buffalo Bill's company has crossed the water several times, that a number of the cowboys have by practice become proficient in riding to hounds, and in steeple-chasing.

SUGGESTED READING

AUCHINCLOSS, LOUIS. *Theodore Roosevelt*. New York: Henry Holt and Company, Inc., 2002.

GRANT, GEORGE E. *Carry a Big Stick: The Uncommon Heroism of Theodore Roosevelt*. Nashville, TN: Cumberland House, 1996.

MCCULLOUGH, DAVID. *Mornings on Horseback*. New York: Simon & Schuster, 1982.

MORRIS, EDMUND. *Rise of Theodore Roosevelt*. New York: Random House, 2001.

ROOSEVELT, THEODORE. *The Man in the Arena: Selected Writings of Theodore Roosevelt*. Ed. Brian M. Thomsen. New York: St. Martin's Press, 2003.

---. *African Game Trails*. New York: St. Martin's Press, 1988.

---. *Autobiography of Theodore Roosevelt*. Cambridge, MA: Da Capo Press, 1985.

---. *Hunting Trips of a Ranchman and The Wilderness Hunter*. New York: Random House, 1996.

---. *Naval War of 1812*. New York: Random House, 1999.

---. *Outdoor Pastimes of an American Hunter*. Harrisburg, PA: Stackpole Books, 1990.

---. *Ranch Life and the Hunting Trail*. Lincoln, NE: University of Nebraska Press, 1983.

---. *Rough Riders*. New York: Random House, 1999.

---. *The Strenuous Life*. Bedford, MA: Applewood Books, 1991.

---. *Through the Brazilian Wilderness*. Lanham, MD: Rowman & Littlefield Publishers, Inc., 2000.

---. *Wilderness Writings.* Layton, UT: Gibbs Smith Books, 1986.

---. *Winning the West Volume 1.* Lincoln, NE: University of Nebraska Press, 1995.

---. *Winning the West Volume 2.* Lincoln, NE: University of Nebraska Press, 1995.

---. *Winning the West Volume 3.* Lincoln, NE: University of Nebraska Press, 1995.

---. *Winning the West Volume 4.* Lincoln, NE: University of Nebraska Press, 1995.

---. *Essential Theodore Roosevelt.* Ed. John Gabriel Hunt. New York: Gramercy, 1994.

---. *Theodore Roosevelt: An American Mind.* Ed. Mario R. Dinunzio. New York: Viking Penguin, 1995.

THAYER, WILLIAM ROSCOE. *Theodore Roosevelt.* New York: Barnes & Noble World Digital Library, 2003.